Rent Control and Leasehold Enfranchisement

Rent Control and Leasehold Enfranchisement

Trevor M Aldridge
MA (Cantab), Solicitor

Eighth Edition

Oyez Publishing Limited

© 1980 Oyez Publishing Limited
Norwich House, 11/13 Norwich Street
London EC4A 1AB

ISBN 0 85120 546 1

First published (as Rent Control and
Security of Tenure)
November, 1965
Revised and Reprinted...January, 1966
New edition (as Rent Control and
Leasehold Enfranchisement)
November, 1967
Third edition ....*September,* 1970
Fourth edition ....*September,* 1972
Fifth edition ....*March,* 1974
Sixth edition ....*May,* 1975
Seventh edition ....*February,* 1977
Eighth edition ....*December,* 1980

Set in Times and Univers by Trident Graphics Ltd
and printed in Great Britain by
Biddles Ltd, Guildford, Surrey

Contents

Preface to the Eighth Edition

Since the publication of the last edition of this book, two major statutes have been passed that affect its contents. First, the Rent Act 1977 again consolidated the provisions of earlier Acts. It made no substantial amendments to the law, but it altered all the references to statutory provisions. Secondly, the Housing Act 1980 changes the law in a number of important ways.

The main effects of the 1980 Act can be summarised in three parts: the changes relating to private sector tenancies; those concerning public sector lettings; and those affecting leasehold enfranchisement. For tenancies granted by private landlords, the Act creates the new categories of protected shorthold tenancies and assured tenancies, and finally abolishes controlled tenancies. It makes it easier for the landlords of various types of tenancy to obtain possession, and it simplifies and accelerates the phasing of rent increases.

The majority of public sector tenants now have security of tenure, as secure tenants. They do not, however, benefit from any rent control.

The adjustments to the leasehold enfranchisement rules are both substantive, making it quicker to qualify to enfranchise, and procedural, substituting leasehold valuation tribunals for the Lands Tribunal.

The Housing Act 1980 provisions about secure tenancies came into force on 3 October 1980, and those concerning assured tenancies on 6 October 1980. The others dealt with in this book await commencement orders. Little delay is expected in making the orders, so the law is stated as it will be when the Act is fully in force. In other respects, this edition seeks to state the law as it stood on 1 October 1980.

9 October 1980   Trevor M Aldridge

Table of Cases

Table of Statutes

Table of Statutory Instruments

Chapter I
Regulated Tenancies

Statutes referred to in this chapter:
Rent Act 1965: '1965 Act.'
Rent Act 1968: '1968 Act.'
Rent (Agriculture) Act 1976: '1976 Act.'
Rent Act 1977: '1977 Act.'
Housing Act 1980: '1980 Act.'

Glossary

All tenancies enjoying full Rent Act protection are now *regulated tenancies*, as the 1980 Act finally abolished the former category of *controlled tenancies* (1980 Act, s 64). Regulated tenancies are divided into two: *protected tenancies* which are contractual tenancies, whether granted for a fixed term or on a periodic basis, and *statutory tenancies* which arise when protected tenancies come to an end.

It is occasionally necessary to distinguish tenancies first brought within the scope of the Rent Act when the rateable value limits were raised on 22 March 1973 from £400 to £600 in Greater London and from £200 to £300 elsewhere (Counter-Inflation Act 1973, s 14). In this book, they are called *higher value regulated tenancies* (which is not a statutory term). Tenancies that became regulated tenancies when the Rent Act 1974 extended the Act to furnished tenancies are called *protected furnished tenancies, regulated furnished tenancies* and *statutory furnished tenancies.*

Protected shorthold tenancies are a subdivision of the category of regulated tenancies, dealt with separately in Chapter III.

A — EXTENT OF CONTROL

1 Qualifications

Subject to the general exceptions dealt with below, a tenancy will be a regulated tenancy (either protected or controlled) if the answer to the following nine questions is Yes.

(1) *Are the premises a dwelling-house?* (1977 Act, s 1)

The term 'dwelling-house' includes part of a house, whether specifically adapted for separate occupation as a home (eg, a flat in a block designed for that purpose) or not (eg, a single room). The fact of residence in premises not designed as a dwelling-house (eg, a lock-up shop) is not sufficient to bring them within the definition. The letting must, however, be as a single dwelling-house, not for multiple occupation (*St Catherine's College* v *Dorling* [1980] 1 WLR 66). A caravan is not included, because of its mobility (*Morgan* v *Taylor* (1948) 99 LJ News 290). The control extends to premises let together with the dwelling-house, eg, a garden and a detached garage, with exceptions in the cases of agricultural land and business premises, which are dealt with separately below. The protection is not prejudiced if, after the letting, the reversion to the dwelling-house and the reversion to the other premises are in the hands of different landlords while the tenant still occupies all that was originally let (*Jelley* v *Buckman* [1974] QB 488).

(2) *Are the premises let without payment for board or attendance?* (1977 Act, ss 1, 7)

The letting must be a true tenancy in law, not eg, occupation by a licensee. This may be a distinction which it is difficult to make and there is much authority on the point. Occupation of a room in a hostel (*R* v *South Middlesex Rent Tribunal, ex parte Beswick* (1976) 32 P & CR 67 or of an almshouse or accommodation in an old people's home will often be unprotected (*Abbeyfield (Harpenden) Society Ltd* v *Woods* [1968] 1 WLR 374). Such lettings may still be restricted contracts (Chapter V). Almspeople may nevertheless qualify for rent allowances. Contractual arrangements made separately with more than one person, under which each is entitled jointly to occupy the whole of the premises – so that none has exclusive possession and there is no joint tenancy – are licences and not protected (*Somma* v *Hazlehurst* [1978] 1 WLR 1014).

For premises to be excluded by reason of payment for attendance, the amount of the rent fairly attributable to it must, having regard to their value to the tenant, form a substantial portion of the whole rent. In one case, on the former equivalent provision concerning payment for furniture, 15½ per cent of the rent was held not to be substantial (*Thomas* v *Pascal* [1969] 1 WLR 1475), but the courts do not favour an exclusively arithmetical approach. Strangely, perhaps, there is no requirement that payment for board should be substantial. 'Board' is not defined, but apparently covers partial board, as long as the amount is not so small as to be disregarded as *de minimis* (*Wilkes* v *Goodwin* [1923] 2 KB 86).

(3) *Are the premises let as a residence without any living accommodation being shared?* (1977 Act, ss 1, 9, 24)

The statutory phrase for premises subject to a protected tenancy is 'a separate dwelling'. The premises must generally be suitable for all normal residential activities, particularly sleeping. For this purpose a corporation cannot be said to reside, and so security of tenure is only given to human tenants, although the benefits of the rent control provisions can apply to corporations (*Carter* v *SU Carburettor Co* [1942] 2 KB 288). Similarly, rent controls benefit tenants not in possession (*Feather Supplies Ltd* v *Ingham* [1971] 2 QB 348).

'Living accommodation' cannot for this purpose be precisely defined. It seems to include rooms which any member of the household uses for any considerable part of the day, rather than just visiting them, so that sharing must necessarily lead to an invasion of privacy.

A letting for the purpose of a holiday cannot be a protected tenancy. There is no definition of holiday purposes. Although not conclusive, the description of a letting in the tenancy agreement as a holiday letting is *prima facie* evidence that it is (*Buchmann* v *May* [1978] 2 All ER 993).

Where the letting is partly for business purposes the control giving security of tenure for business tenancies (Landlord and Tenant Act 1954, Pt II) may apply, but it is outside the scope of this book (see Aldridge, *Letting Business Premises*). It applies if the business use is something more than minimal (*Cheryl Investments Ltd* v *Saldanha; Royal Life Saving Society* v *Page* [1978] 1 WLR 1329). If the 1954 Act applies, the letting cannot be a regulated tenancy.

(4) *Is the rent at least two-thirds of the rateable value of the premises?* (1977 Act, ss 5, 25 (3); 1980 Act, Sched 8, para 1)

With two exceptions, the rateable value considered is that on 23 March 1965, or the first day thereafter when the premises appeared in the valuation list. Premises with a rateable value over £400 in Greater London, or £200 elsewhere, before 22 March 1973, constitute one exception. For them, the comparison is with rateable value on 22 March 1973. For lettings by the Duchies of Lancaster and Cornwall and the Crown Estate Commissioners, the rateable value is that at the commencement date of s 73 of the 1980 Act.

In comparing the rent payable under tenancies granted for over twenty-one years with the rateable value, there must be disregarded any sums payable by the tenant, however expressed, for rates, services, repairs, maintenance or insurance, unless the parties could not have regarded it as a part payable for those purposes. In other cases, the rent for the purposes of this comparison is everything paid to the landlord, even if the rent is inclusive of, eg, rates (*Sydney Trading Co* v *Finsbury Borough Council* [1952] 1 All ER 460).

The rent must be in money, not services (*Barnes* v *Barratt* [1970] 2 QB 657), unless an agreed rent is set off against an agreed salary, when the whole rent counts (*Montagu* v *Browning* [1954] 1 WLR 1039).

(5) *Is the immediate landlord someone other than the Crown or one of the bodies listed below?* (1977 Act, ss 13–16; 1980 Act, ss 73, 74; Protected Tenancies (Exceptions) Regulations 1974; Protected Tenancies (Further Exceptions) Regulations 1976)

For this purpose the Crown extends to interests enjoyed by government departments, and to those held in trust for the purposes, of government departments, but does not include the interests of the Duchies of Lancaster and Cornwall, nor those managed by the Crown Estate Commissioners.

The other 'exempted bodies' are:

(i) County and district councils, the Common Council of the City of London, London borough councils and the Greater London Council.

(ii) Development corporations for new towns and the Commission for the New Towns.

(iii) Registered housing associations (Housing Act 1974, s 18 (1)). This is a double requirement: the landlord must be an association as defined by the Housing Act 1957, s 189 (1) (as amended by the Housing Act 1974, Sched 13, para 6) and must be registered under the Housing Act 1974, s 13.

The definition of a housing association includes the Church of England Pensions Board (Clergy Pensions Measure 1961, s 29).

The condition of registration does not apply to an association:

(a) registered under the Industrial and Provident Societies Act 1965, whose rules restrict membership to tenants and tenancies to members (ie, co-ownership associations or societies); or

(b) specified in a ministerial order applying to it provisions relating to local authorities.

(iv) Housing trusts (defined, pp 86–7).

(v) The Housing Corporation.

(vi) A co-operative, exercising local authority housing functions (Housing Rents and Subsidies Act 1975, Sched 5, para 1).

(vii) Certain educational institutions. The following institutions are included, and any corporate body or unincorporated body of persons by whom any such institution is provided. This exemption only applies where the tenancy is granted to a person pursuing or intending to pursue a course of study provided by one of the following bodies, even though the landlord may be a different body:

(a) any university, university college, or constituent college, school or hall of a university;

(b) any further education establishment for which grants are paid under the Further Education Regulations 1975, reg 19 (1) (b);

(c) any further education establishment designated as a polytechnic and assisted by a local education authority under a scheme approved under the Education Act 1944, s 42.

(viii) Certain named organisations providing student accommodation. They are: Birmingham Friendship Housing Association; Bishop Creighton House, London; Carrs Lane Chapel, Birmingham; Hamtun Housing Association Ltd, Southampton; Hull Students' Welfare Association; International Students' Housing Society, Woolwich; International Students' Trust, London; London House for Overseas Graduates, London; Oxford Overseas Student Housing Association Ltd; St Thomas More Housing Society Ltd, Oxford; Student Homes Ltd, London; Victoria League for Commonwealth Friendship, London; Wandsworth Students' Housing Association Ltd; and York Housing Association Ltd.

(6) *Is the landlord resident elsewhere than in another part of the building?* (1977 Act, s 12)

The tenant of a resident landlord has the protection of the rent tribunal. The detailed rules for determining whether a letting is in this category are set out in Chapter IV,

(7) *If the house is let together with agricultural land, is the area of that land two acres or less?* (1977 Act, s 26)

(8) *Is the rateable value within any of the following limits?* (1977 Act, s 4)

Rateable value on	Premises in Greater London	Elsewhere
23 March 1965	£400	£200
22 March 1973	£600	£300
1 April 1973	£1,500	£750

If the premises were first entered in the valuation list after 23 March 1965, the date of that entry should be substituted for the next earlier date in the table. Premises need only fall within one of these limits for the answer to this question to be Yes.

An alteration to the rateable value taking effect between the dates in the table does not affect the position, even if accompanied by a repayment of rates in respect of an earlier period (*Rodwell* v *Gwynne Trusts Ltd* [1970] 1 WLR 327).

Premises are deemed to be within the rateable value limits

unless the contrary is shown and this entitles a rent officer to assume jurisdiction where he believes that premises without a separate rateable value would be within the limits if an apportionment were made (*R* v *Westminster (City) London Borough Rent Officer, ex parte Rendall* [1973] QB 959). Disputes can be referred to the county court.

(9) *Is the tenancy outside the category of assured tenancies?*
(1977 Act, s 16A; 1980 Act, s 56 (5))

Premises that are subject to an assured tenancy (Chapter VIII) cannot be subject to a regulated tenancy.

2 Exceptions

Notwithstanding the replies to the foregoing questions, if the answer to any of the following three questions is Yes, the tenancy cannot be regulated.

(10) *Have the premises an on-licence?* (1977 Act, s 11)

Premises consisting of, or comprising, premises licensed for the sale of intoxicating liquor for consumption on the premises cannot be let on a protected tenancy. It should be noted that this goes wider than public houses. Many hotels, restaurants and clubs now have liquor licences of a restricted type (Licensing Act 1964, Pt IV), which are nevertheless on-licences. An off-licence affords no automatic exemption, but premises with both on- and off-licences, as most public houses have, are not subject to control. Most lettings of premises with off-licences will not be regulated tenancies because the Landlord and Tenant Act 1954, Pt II, will apply to them.

(11) *Are the premises an agricultural holding occupied by the person responsible for the control of the farming of it?*
(1977 Act, s 10)

An agricultural holding is defined as 'the aggregate of the agricultural land comprised in a contract of tenancy, not being a contract under which the said land is let to the tenant during his continuance in any office, appointment or employment under the landlord' (Agricultural Holdings Act 1948, s 1 (1)). The control of the farming may be as tenant, or as servant or agent of the tenant.

(12) *Are the premises a parsonage house?*

Each benefice of the Church of England normally has a parsonage house, which is part of the endowment of the benefice and owned by the incumbent as a corporation sole. It is generally the incumbent's duty to live there, but in certain circumstances he is permitted to let it (Pluralities Act 1838, s 59). In this event the letting is outside all controls dealt with in this book (*Bishop of Gloucester* v *Cunnington* [1943] KB 101). This exemption extends to a cottage belonging to the benefice which is separate from, but necessary for the convenient occupation of the parsonage house (*Culverwell* v *Larcombe* [1946] KB 243). In possession proceedings the fact that a parsonage house is totally exempt from control means that it is immaterial that the intention in evicting the tenant is not reoccupation by the incumbent, but simply reletting at an increased rent (*Brandon* v *Grundy* [1943] 2 All ER 208). Other ministers of religion have qualified rights to recover possession of houses let on regulated tenancies (pp 25–6).

B — RENT TO BE CHARGED

1 Registered rent

While a rent for premises let on a regulated tenancy is registered, that registered rent automatically is, subject to the variations explained below and to the phasing restrictions, the maximum rent recoverable (1977 Act, s 44 (1)). This applies equally if the registration is in other parts of the register, relating to housing association lettings or statutory tenancies of agricultural tied cottages (1977 Act, s 87 (6); 1976 Act, s 13 (7)).

The position is similar where a rent for a regulated furnished tenancy had been registered by a rent tribunal before the tenancy became protected, or while the resident landlord control applied. That registered rent constitutes the maximum recoverable rent until a fair rent is registered by the rent officer (1977 Act, Sched 24, para 8). On the other hand, a rent registered for an unfurnished letting before furnished lettings were regulated does not limit rent payable under a regulated furnished tenancy (*Metrobarn Ltd* v *Gehring* [1976] 1 WLR 776).

A transitional provision ensures that for a higher value regulated tenancy, the rent legally recoverable on 22 March 1973 is not reduced by a subsequent registration (1977 Act, Sched 7, paras 1, 2).

A registered rent takes effect from the date that the rent officer's decision is registered, or on appeal from the date the rent assessment committee makes its decision (1977 Act, s 72 (1)–(3); 1980 Act, s 61). If a registered rent is confirmed by the rent officer, the confirmation takes effect when noted on the register. If it is confirmed by the rent assessment committee it takes effect when the committee makes its decision There is one exception. Where the landlord exercises his right to apply for a reassessment of the rent within the last three months of the two-year period that a registration normally lasts, the new registration does not take effect until the end of the former two years. That period is three years, rather than two, in the case of a registration before s 60 of the 1980 Act took effect.

The effective date is given on the register, and each registration supersedes the previous one from that date (1977 Act, s 72 (4), (5); 1980 Act, s 61). The provisions as to registration and applications to change registered rents are dealt with in the next Chapter.

In two cases the registered rent may be subject to automatic variation without amendment of the register. These are the payment of rates, and payments for services, maintenance and repairs. In each case the position must be made clear on the register.

(a) Where rates are borne by the landlord, or a superior landlord, these are to be added to the registered rent. During any statutory period of a regulated tenancy for which the rent is registered no notices of increase are required (1977 Act, s 72 (2), (3)).

(b) The terms of a regulated tenancy may provide for the tenant to pay the landlord variable sums for services provided by, or for works of maintenance or repair carried out by, the landlord or a superior landlord. Where the variation is according to the cost from time to time of the services or works, and the rent officer or the rent assessment committee is satisfied that the terms as to variation are reasonable, the rent may be entered in the register as variable in accordance with those terms (1977 Act, s 71 (4)).

A valid notice of increase served on the tenant before registration may authorise a rent higher than the amount of the subsequent registration. In such a case that notice is only valid so far as it increases the rent up to the registered rent, and the excess is irrecoverable (1977 Act, s 72 (6); 1980 Act, s 61).

2 Contractual tenancies if no registered rent

Where there is no subsisting entry on the register of rents, the recoverable rent depends upon to which of the following two questions the answer is Yes.

(1) *Are the premises vacant?*

There is no limit to what may be charged. The tenant's safeguard is that he may always apply to have a fair rent registered.

(2) *Are the premises occupied by a sitting tenant?*

The rent under a subsisting regulated tenancy can only be increased, in the absence of an application for registration, by a 'rent agreement with a tenant having security of tenure.' This term includes both an agreement increasing the rent payable under a regulated tenancy and the grant of a new tenancy at a higher rent to the sitting tenant, or a person who might succeed him as statutory tenant (1977 Act, s 51 (1)). An increase in rent merely to cover an increase in rates borne by the landlord or a superior landlord does not require a rent agreement.

The rent agreement must (1977 Act, s 51 (4); 1980 Act, s 68 (1)) –

    (i) be in writing signed by both parties; and

    (ii) be headed by a statement, in characters no less conspicuous than those used in any other part of the agreement (which means 'equally readable': *Middlegate Properties Ltd* v *Messimeris* [1973] 1 WLR 168), to the following effect: that the tenant's security of tenure under the 1977 Act will not be prejudiced if he refuses to enter into it; that if a rent were registered instead of the agreement being made, only part of any increase would be payable during the first year; and that the agreement will not deprive either party of the right at any time to apply to the rent officer for the registration of a fair rent.

Any overpayment of rent resulting from non-compliance with these formalities can only be recovered within one year after payment, instead of the usual two years (1977 Act, s 57 (3) *(a)*; 1980 Act, s 68 (3)).

Special rules apply in the case of former controlled tenancies which were converted into regulated tenancies (see next section).

3 Converted tenancies

A rent agreement with a tenant having security of tenure raising the rent payable under a former controlled tenancy is only valid if a rent is registered for the premises (1977 Act, s 52; 1980 Act, s 68 (2)). The conversion of the controlled tenancy must have been under one of the following provisions:

(a) Qualification certificate procedure (Housing Finance Act 1972, Pt III; Housing Act 1969, s 43; 1977 Act, Pt VIII);

(b) Second statutory succession (1968 Act, Sched 2, para 5; 1977 Act, s 18 (3));

(c) Conversion where premises exceeded a specified rateable value (Housing Finance Act 1972, Pt IV);

(d) Conversion of all remaining controlled tenancies (1980 Act, s 64 (1)).

Rent agreements are only affected if the tenant they are made with was the tenant under the controlled tenancy when it was converted, or someone to whom that tenancy could have been transmitted had he then died.

An agreement merely raising the rent is void if no rent is registered when it is made. An agreement which grants a new regulated tenancy is effective, but until a rent is registered, the rent recoverable under it is limited to the amount recoverable under the former tenancy.

4 Statutory tenancies when rent is not registered

If no rent has been registered, the maximum rent recoverable for any statutory period of a regulated tenancy is the rent recoverable for the last contractual rental period of that tenancy, except in the case of a statutory tenancy arising on the termination of a long tenancy at a low rent (1967 Act, Sched 5, para 3 (2) *(b)*). The rent may be raised without registering it if a rent agreement is entered into complying with the statutory requirements. This turns the tenancy back into a contractual one. The maximum for the statutory period is to be varied as follows:

(a) Rates. Where the rates are borne by the landlord, or a superior landlord, or were so borne during the last contractual period, the rent is to be increased by the amount of any difference between the current amount of the rates and the amount for the last contractual period (1977 Act, s 46 (1)). No increase can take effect unless a notice of increase, on Form No 1 (1977 Act, ss 46 (2), 49 (2)), is served by the landlord on the tenant. The notice must specify the amount of the increase and the date when it takes effect. The effective date cannot be earlier than six weeks before the service of the notice. If the notice does take effect before the service of the notice, arrears become due on the day after service (1977 Act, s 46 (2), (3)).

(b) Services and furniture. Where the landlord or a superior landlord provides services for the tenant, or the tenant has the use of furniture, the rent is to be increased or decreased by an amount appropriate to reflect any change in the circumstances relating thereto since the last contractual period. The change must be such as to affect the amount of rent that it is reasonable to charge (1977 Act, s 47 (1)). Any question as to whether or by how much the rent should be adjusted on this ground is to be determined by written agreement between the landlord and the tenant, or by the county court. The determination may relate to past statutory periods and continues until revoked, or varied by agreement or by the county court (1977 Act, s 47 (2)).

Where the regulated tenancy is converted from a controlled tenancy, the comparison under paragraphs *(a)* and *(b)* above is made not with the last contractual period but with the last rental period beginning before conversion (1977 Act, Sched 17, para 2).

For statutory tenancies arising on the termination of a long tenancy at a low rent, the variations under paragraphs *(a)* and *(b)* above apply only if the rent is arrived at by agreement. The comparison is then with the first statutory period, rather than the last contractual period (1967 Act, Sched 5, para 3 (2) *(c)*).

5 Statutory tenancies when rent registered

If the rent recoverable during the statutory period before registration exceeds the rent which is registered (as restricted by phasing if appropriate), the excess is irrecoverable from the effective date of registration, notwithstanding anything in any agreement (1977 Act, s 45 (2) (a)). If the registered rent is higher than the previous statutory rent, the latter may be increased up to the registered limit, subject to the provisions for phasing rent increases. The landlord must serve notice of increase in Form No 3 on the tenant specifying the date when the increase will be effective. It cannot be backdated more than four weeks, or (if less than four weeks earlier) before the date of registration (1977 Act, s 45 (2) (b), (3)). There is no necessity for a notice of increase to take effect on a day for payment of rent (*Avenue Properties (St John's Wood) Ltd* v *Aisinzon* [1977] QB 628).

6 Phasing rent increases

In most cases where an increased rent is registered, the amount recoverable from the tenant is only raised in stages (1977 Act, s 55).

For phasing to apply, the tenancy must fall into one of three categories: it must have been subsisting on 10 March 1975; or, it must have been subsisting on the date of registration of the rent; or, it must have been granted after registration to someone who was then a regulated tenant, a statutory tenant under the 1976 Act, or might have been a successor of either of them by statutory transmission.

Phasing permits the rent to rise in two steps (1977 Act, Sched 8; 1980 Act, s 60 (3)). As soon as a higher rent is registered, the whole of any increase in any part of the rent attributable to services can be charged. That increase is called 'the service element'. In addition, half the remaining difference between the previous recoverable rent and the registered rent may be charged. The full rent may be charged at the end of the first year. The year runs from the date the registration takes effect, ie, from the date the rent officer's decision was registered or the date the rent assessment committee took its decision. So, an appeal to the rent assessment committee delays both the date that a new rent takes effect and the date the landlord can recover the full amount of it.

Example:
1 Old registered rent: £15 per week (of which £3 attributable to services).
2 New registered rent: £21 per week (of which £5 attributable to services).
3 Service element: £5 − £3 = £2.
4 New rent immediately: £15 (old rent) + £2 (service element) + £2 (½ balance of £4) = £19 per week.
5 Rent on first anniversary: £19 + £2 (second half of balance) = £21 per week (full registered rent).

The first year's rent can be arrived at by adding the previous rent limit *(P)*, the service element *(S)* and the new registered rent *(R)*, and halving the total.

First year's rent $= \frac{1}{2}(P+S+R)$.

Where the proportion of the previous registered rent attributable to services was registered, there will be no difficulty in calculating the service element. Where that was not done, it is arrived at as follows (1977 Act, Sched 8, para 2). If the rent officer or the rent assessment committee considers that no part of the previous rent was attributable to services, the service element is the whole of the sum now so attributed. In any other case, it is assumed that the payment for services formed the same proportion of the old rent as is the case for the new one. The amount of the service element is registered.

A new rent may be registered before the previous phasing has expired. In that case, the new phasing takes effect by treating the rent then recoverable as the base from which the phasing starts, rather than the full previous registered rent (1977 Act, Sched 8, para 4). So, taking the facts of the example above, assume a new rent was registered during the first year, when the recoverable rent was £19 per week. In doing the calculation with the new figures, the sum in step 1 ('old registered rent'), would be £19 per week (of which £5 is attributable to services).

A notice of increase served on a tenant which specifies a rent higher than is properly recoverable under these phasing provisions takes effect as if it only required payment of the correct sum (1977 Act, s 55 (2)).

7 Amount of rates

Where the amount of rates paid in a particular period is relevant in computing a rent, there are general rules for calculating those rates. 'Rates' includes water rates and charges, but excludes owner's drainage rates (1977 Act, s 152 (1)).

The amount of rates attributable to any rental period is the same proportion of the total rates for the rating period as the length of the rental period bears to the length of the rating period (1977 Act, Sched 5, para 1). For example, if rates are charged annually and rent is paid weekly, the rates must be divided by $52^1/_7$ ($52^2/_7$ in leap years) for each rental period. Any discount allowed to the landlord in paying the rates is not passed on to the tenant (1977 Act, Sched 5, para 5). Where the premises form part only of a hereditament assessed for rating purposes, the amount of rates is a proportion of the amount charged on the whole hereditament. The proportion is to be agreed in writing between the landlord and the tenant, or determined by the county court (1977 Act, s 75 (2)).

8 Comparison of differing rental periods

Where rents or rates payable in two different rental periods have to be compared, and those rental periods are of different lengths, the necessary adjustment must be made. For this purpose, one month is to be treated as equal to one-twelfth of a year, and a week as equal to one fifty-second part of a year (1977 Act, s 59).

9 Excess rent

Amounts of rent over the maxima specified above are irrecoverable from the tenant. If any irrecoverable amounts have been paid they can be recovered from the landlord or his personal representative, by deduction from future payments of rent as well as by any other means (1977 Act, s 57). There is a time limit for the recovery of overpayments. This is one year in the case of non-compliance with the formalities for a rent agreement with a tenant having security of tenure, and two years in other cases (1977 Act, s 57(3); 1980 Act, s 68 (3)).

Any person making an entry in a rent book or similar document showing a tenant in arrear in respect of any irrecoverable sum is guilty of an offence. A landlord who does not delete such an entry within seven days of being so requested is similarly guilty. An offender is liable on summary conviction to a fine of up to £50, unless he proves a bona fide claim to the sum shown (1977 Act, s 57 (4), (5)).

C — SECURITY OF TENURE

A statutory tenancy arises on the termination of a contractual protected tenancy where the tenant (or even the survivor of joint tenants: *Lloyd* v *Sadler* [1978] QB 774) remains in possession. Statutory tenants are entitled to continue to occupy the premises comprised in their former contractual tenancy upon the same terms, so far as they are not inconsistent with the Rent Act (1977 Act, s 3 (1)). The original contractual tenant therefore enjoys complete security of tenure unless the contractual tenancy is assigned by operation of law (eg, on bankruptcy: *Smalley* v *Quarrier* [1975] 1 WLR 938), the statutory tenancy comes to an end, or the landlord makes a successful application to the county court for an order for possession. Such an application would have to be founded on one of the grounds for possession discussed in the next section.

A deserted wife's occupation of the matrimonial home counts as her husband's possession (Matrimonial Homes Act 1967, s 1 (5)), but a deserted mistress has no analogous right (*Colin Smith Music Ltd* v *Ridge* [1975] 1 WLR 463). Before a contractual tenancy comes to an end, it may be transferred from one spouse to another on divorce under the Matrimonial Causes Act 1973, s 24, except, possibly, if the terms of the tenancy prohibit assignment (*Hale* v *Hale* [1975] 1 WLR 931).

Even if an order for possession of premises within the scope of the control is made, the court has wide powers to qualify it (1977 Act, s 100; 1980 Act, s 75 (1)–(3)). The court may adjourn the application, stay or suspend execution or postpone the date of possession for such period or periods as it thinks fit. It must impose conditions as to payment of rent, including arrears or mesne profits, unless that would cause the tenant exceptional hardship or would otherwise be unreasonable. The court may also impose such other conditions as it thinks fit. This jurisdiction càn be exercised in favour of the tenant's spouse or former spouse, who is occupying the premises under rights conferred by the Matrimonial Homes Act 1967. On compliance with the conditions imposed, the court may discharge or rescind the order.

1 Termination of statutory tenancy

The statutory tenancy can come to an end in any of the following ways:

(*a*) if the tenant gives up possession, unless his spouse continues in occupation and pays the rent (Matrimonial Homes Act 1967, s 1 (5)), or no longer uses the premises as his residence. It is for the landlord to prove that the tenant is no longer resident (*Roland House Gardens Ltd* v *Cravitz* (1975) 29 P & CR 432). In some circumstances, the statutory tenancy will continue even if the tenant spends most of his time in another residence abroad (*Bevington* v *Crawford* (1974) 232 EG 191), or if the tenant has not occupied the premises for ten years (*Gofor Investments Ltd* v *Roberts* (1975) 29 P & CR 366);

(*b*) if the tenant surrenders the tenancy by operation of law (*Collins* v *Claughton* [1959] 1 WLR 145);

(*c*) if the premises cease to exist (*Ellis & Sons Amalgamated Properties Ltd* v *Sisman* [1948] 1 KB 653);

(*d*) if the landlord by consent alters the premises and reduces the rent below two-thirds of the appropriate rateable value (*McKenna* v *Baker* (1959) 1973 EG 441);

(*e*) if the tenant changes the nature of his occupation (eg, from tenant to purchaser: *Turner* v *Watts* (1928) 97 LJKB 403); or

(*f*) if a new contractual tenancy is granted to the tenant (*Bungalows (Maidenhead) Ltd* v *Mason* [1954] 1 WLR 769).

2 Transfer of statutory tenancy by divorce court order

A court hearing a divorce or nullity petition where one spouse is a statutory tenant, or they both are jointly, may, between the date of granting the decree nisi and its being made absolute, order that the other spouse, or one only of the spouses, be the statutory tenant (Matrimonial Homes Act 1967, s 7 (3)). The former statutory tenant's rights then terminate as from the date of the decree absolute.

3 Transmission of statutory tenancy

On the death of a statutory tenant, the tenancy may be transmitted twice, but no more, to one of a limited class of people (1977 Act, Sched 1).

There is an exception in the case of a tenancy of an agricultural tied cottage, let on what would have been a protected occupancy had that tenancy, or a previous tenancy to that tenant or a member of his family, been at a low rent. In that case, there is only one statutory transmission, if the original tenancy was granted on or after 1 January 1977 (or, in the case of forestry workers, 1 October 1977) (1977 Act, Sched 1, para 11).

Primarily the transmission is to the tenant's surviving spouse if residing in the premises immediately before the tenant's death. For the second transmission, references to the deceased 'tenant' must be construed as applying to the person who took the statutory tenancy on the first transmission. If the tenant leaves no such surviving spouse, the tenancy may be transmitted to such member of the tenant's family who was residing with him or her for not less than six months immediately before his death as is agreed. In default of agreement the county court decides (1977 Act, Sched 1, paras 1–7; 1980 Act, s 76 (1), (2)). To reside with the tenant means to share the whole premises as a member of the household on a reasonably permanent basis. Although the word 'family' is usually confined here to blood relations and in-laws, it can extend further, eg to a spinster with whom the tenant lived as man and wife for forty years (*Dyson Holdings Ltd* v *Fox* [1976] QB 503), but it does not cover the informal adoption of an aunt-nephew relationship (*Carega Properties SA* v *Sharratt* [1979] 1 WLR 928). The agreement as to which member of the family takes the tenancy is to be made between the members of the family: the landlord is not concerned.

A tenancy granted after 27 August 1972 to someone who is already the first or second successor to a statutory tenancy of those premises does not give rise to the new succession rights that a new tenancy would normally confer (1977 Act, Sched 1, para 10). Were this not so, landlords could not safely raise the rent by agreement in such cases. Accordingly, the new tenancy can only be transmitted once if the tenant is himself a first successor, and not at all if he is a second successor.

Special transitional provisions apply to a regulated furnished tenancy of which the tenant died before 14 August 1974 (1977 Act, Sched 24, para 7 (5)). If the person who was in possession on that day could have been a first successor, he became a statutory tenant and was deemed to be the first successor.

If the statutory tenancy has been transferred in the course of a divorce or nullity case, as explained in the previous section, it is counted as continuous for this purpose, and any transmission before the transfer order counts towards the maximum of two that are allowed (Matrimonial Homes Act 1967, s 7 (3)).

4 Sub-tenants

Where the tenant is a lawful sub-tenant whose immediate landlord himself enjoys statutory protection, the sub-tenant has some protection if the head tenancy comes to an end (1977 Act, s 137). The head tenant's protection may have been as a protected or statutory tenant, under the 1976 Act or, if the sub-tenancy would have been protected by the 1976 Act had it been at a low rent, under the Agricultural Holdings Act 1948.

On the head tenancy of a dwelling-house coming to an end, the sub-tenant becomes the direct tenant of the head landlord, on the terms that applied to the sub-tenancy. Where the head lease comprised more than a dwelling-house the sub-letting continues as if there had originally been separate lettings of the dwelling-house and the remainder of the premises. This applies where the head lease was of an agricultural holding, if the sub-tenancy is one that the 1976 Act would have protected had it reserved a low rent.

A possession order terminating the head tenancy on any of the discretionary grounds for possession does not upset the sub-tenant's right to possession.

This protection applies also to sub-tenants whose immediate landlord holds under a long tenancy at a low rent, with two exceptions. A sub-tenancy is not protected if, at the date it was created, either the landlord had already given notice to terminate the long tenancy, or the long tenancy would by then already have expired, but for the fact that the Landlord and Tenant Act 1954 Pt I, had extended it pending the service of notice.

D — GROUNDS FOR POSSESSION

1 Discretionary grounds

There is an overriding requirement, before an order for possession is made on one of the following grounds, that the court must think it reasonable to do so (1977 Act, s 98 (1)). Therefore, even if one of the grounds is established, the court must still have regard to the surrounding circumstances.

The grounds for possession are (1977 Act, Sched 15, Pt I):

(a) Case 1: Breach of obligation. Non-payment of rent lawfully due, or a breach of an obligation of the tenancy (whether contractual or statutory).

(b) Case 2: Nuisance, annoyance, etc. Any of the following acts on the part of the tenant, any person residing or lodging with him, or a sub-tenant:

(i) conduct which is a nuisance or annoyance to adjoining occupiers;

(ii) conviction for using or allowing the premises to be used for immoral or illegal purposes. The landlord must show that the premises were specifically used for crime, rather than merely that the crime happened to be committed there (*Abrahams* v *Wilson* [1971] 2 QB 88).

(c) Cases 3 and 4: Dilapidations. Deterioration in the condition of the premises or of the furniture provided for use under the tenancy. This must have been caused by the tenant, any person residing or lodging with him or a sub-tenant. In the case of the premises, it must be the result of waste, or neglect or default, and in the case of the furniture, the result of ill treatment.

Where the acts concerned are those of a lodger or sub-tenant, the court must be satisfied that the tenant has not taken such steps as he reasonably ought to remove the offender.

(d) Case 5: Tenant's notice to quit. In consequence of the tenant having given notice to quit, the landlord has contracted to sell or let the premises or taken some other step whereby he would be seriously prejudiced if he did not obtain possession.

(e) Case 6: Assignment or total sub-letting. Assigning or sub-letting the whole of the premises, or the part not previously sub-let, without the landlord's consent. This must have taken place after the following dates:

higher value regulated tenancies: 22 March 1973;

regulated furnished tenancies: 14 August 1974;

Duchy of Lancaster, Duchy of Cornwall and Crown Estate Commissioners lettings: the commencement date of s 73 of the 1980 Act (1980 Act, Sched 8, para 2);

all other cases: 8 December 1965.

(f) Case 8: Employee's accommodation. The landlord reasonably requiring the premises for the residence of a whole-time employee of the landlord, or of a tenant of his.

A contract for such employment, conditional on having accommodation, with the person for whom the premises are required suffices. This ground only applies where the tenant was formerly in the employment of the landlord, or a former landlord, and the house was let to him in consequence of that employment. It is not available to recover possession of an agricultural tied cottage, where the tenancy would have been a protected occupancy or 1976 Act statutory tenancy, had the tenancy or an earlier tenancy granted to that tenant or a member of his family been at a low rent (1977 Act, s 99 (2)).

(g) Case 9: Own occupation. The landlord reasonably requiring the premises as a residence for himself, or any son or daughter of his over eighteen years old, or his father or mother, or the mother or father of his spouse.

To this there are two qualifications. First, the ground is not available to a landlord who purchased the house, or any interest in it, with a sitting tenant so becoming landlord (*Fowle* v *Bell* [1947] KB 242), after the following dates:

higher value regulated tenancies: 8 March 1973;

regulated furnished tenancies: 24 May 1974;

all other cases: 23 March 1965.

Secondly, no order is to be made where the court considers that greater hardship would be caused by making it than by refusing it. One only of two joint landlords requiring the premises for himself does not come within this ground for possession (*McIntyre* v *Hardcastle* [1948] 2 KB 82).

(*h*) *Case 10: Sub-letting at excess rent.* Charging a sub-tenant (where the sub-letting is also regulated) more than the recoverable rent for the sub-let premises.

(*i*) *Suitable alternative accommodation* (1977 Act, s 98 (1) (*a*), (4), Sched 15, Pt IV).

It is for the landlord to prove that suitable alternative accommodation for the tenant is, or will when the possession order takes effect be, available. There are two ways open to him. Either he can produce a certificate from the housing authority for the area in which the premises are situated, to the effect that it will produce suitable alternative accommodation by a certain date. This is conclusive. Or the landlord must prove that accommodation is or will be available that complies with the following conditions:

(i) it will be let on a regulated tenancy (unless the landlord under it might recover possession on one of the mandatory grounds: 1980 Act, Sched 25, para 58), or on terms affording reasonably equivalent security;

(ii) that, in the opinion of the court, it is reasonably suitable to the needs of the tenant and his family as regards proximity to place of work; and

(iii) either that it is similar in rental and accommodation to premises provided in the neighbourhood by any housing authority for those whose needs in extent of accommodation are similar to those of the tenant and his family, or that it is otherwise reasonably suitable to the tenant's means and the needs of him and his family in extent and character. This includes environmental considerations (*Redspring Ltd* v *Francis* [1973] 1 WLR 134). If furniture was provided under the subsisting tenancy, furniture must be provided in the alternative accommodation which is either similar or reasonably suitable to the needs of the tenant and his family. Part only of what the tenant occupies may be suitable alternative (*Mykolyshyn* v *Noah* [1970] 1 WLR 1271).

Where an agricultural tied cottage is let on a tenancy that would have been protected by the 1976 Act had it been at a low rent, provisions equivalent to cases I and II under the 1976 Act apply (1977 Act, Sched 16).

2 Mandatory grounds

If the landlord establishes one of the following grounds, he is entitled to an order for possession, and the judge has no further discretion (1977 Act, Sched 15, Pt II).

Relevant date. In a number of these cases, a notice has to be served by the relevant date. The relevant date is (1977 Act, Sched 15, Pt III, para 2; 1980 Act, Sched 8, para 3):

Regulated tenancies subsisting on 14 August 1974: 13 February 1975.

Higher value regulated tenancies subsisting on 22 March 1973: 22 September 1973.

Tenancies granted by the Duchy of Lancaster, the Duchy of Cornwall or the Crown Estate Commissioners and subsisting when s 73 of the 1980 Act came into force: 8 February 1981.

Other tenancies subsisting on 8 December 1965: 7 June 1966.

All other regulated tenancies: the date of commencement of that tenancy.

(a) Case 11: Owner-occupier. The landlord who let the premises ('owner-occupier') formerly lived there, and possession is required in one of the following circumstances (1980 Act, s 66 (1), Sched 7):

(i) as a residence for the owner-occupier (including one only of two joint owners: *Tilling* v *Whiteman* [1980] AC 1) or any member of his family who resided with him when he was last there. The requirement of possession for reoccupation must be genuine, but need not be reasonable (*Kennealy* v *Dunne* [1977] QB 837);

(ii) if the tenancy was granted and the owner-occupier died after s 66 of the 1980 Act came into force: first, as a residence for a member of his family who resided with him when he died; and secondly, as a residence for a successor in title who is not, and does not claim through, a purchaser for value; or thirdly, so that the premises may be sold with vacant possession;

(iii) a mortgagee, under a mortgage by deed made before the tenancy was granted, is entitled to exercise a statutory or contractual power of sale, and requires to sell with vacant possession;

(iv) when the premises are not reasonably suitable to the owner-occupier's needs having regard to his place of work, to use the proceeds of sale with vacant possession to buy premises which are more suitable.

The landlord must, not later than the relevant date, have given the tenant written notice that possession might be required under this Case (formerly 1965 Act, s 14 or 1968 Act, Sched 3, Case 10).

In the case of a regulated furnished tenancy, notice served before 14 August 1974 under the 1968 Act, s 79 (the equivalent provision formerly applying to furnished lettings) suffices.

The claimant landlord must have served notice for all regulated tenancies that he granted since 8 December 1965, or (for higher value regulated tenancies) since 22 March 1973, or (for regulated furnished tenancies) since 14 August 1974. The court may dispense with the requirements of notice on the current or previous tenants if it is just and equitable to make an order for possession.

In a case where all notices have been duly given, or the court is asked to waive the requirement for notice to be served on a former tenant, but not the current one, the landlord may use a summary procedure to apply for possession (Rent (County Court Proceedings) (Case 11) Rules 1978).

(b) Case 12: Retirement home. The premises were let, before his retirement, by an owner who intends to occupy them on retirement from regular employment, and possession is required in one of the following circumstances (1980 Act, s 66 (2), (4), Sched 7):

(i) as a residence for the landlord who has retired from regular employment;

(ii) after the landlord's death, as a residence for a member of his family who resided with him when he died;

(iii) if the tenancy was granted and the landlord died after s 66 of the 1980 Act came into force, as a residence for a successor in title, who neither is nor claims through a purchaser for value, or for sale with vacant possession;

(iv) a mortgagee, under a mortgage by deed made before the tenancy was granted, is entitled to exercise a statutory or contractual power of sale, and requires to sell with vacant possession.

The landlord must have given the tenant written notice, not later than the relevant date, that possession might be required under this Case (formerly 1968 Act, Sched 3, Case 10A). All lettings since 14 August 1974 must have been subject to such a notice. The requirements about notice may be waived if the court considers it just and equitable to make a possession order.

(c) Case 13: Holiday premises let off season. The premises were formerly used as holiday accommodation. The letting must be for a term certain not exceeding eight months, and the premises must have been occupied under a right to occupy them for a holiday (not necessarily a tenancy) within twelve months ending on the relevant date. A tenancy is, for this purpose, for a term certain notwithstanding a liability to determination on re-entry, or any other event except the landlord giving notice. Although no doubt intended to facilitate the letting of holiday accommodation out of season, this ground may be used at any time of year.

The landlord must, not later than the relevant date, give the tenant written notice that possession might be recovered under this Case (formerly 1968 Act, Sched 3, Case 10B).

(d) Case 14: Former student accommodation. The premises were formerly student accommodation. The letting must be for a term certain not exceeding twelve months, and during the twelve months ending on the relevant date they must have been let by an educational institution, or one of the named organisations providing student accommodation, on a tenancy which is for that reason not regulated (pp 5–6). A tenancy is for a term certain notwithstanding a liability to determination on re-entry, or on any other event except the landlord giving notice.

(e) Case 15: Minister of religion's house. Premises held for the purpose of being available for occupation by a minister of religion as a residence from which to perform his duties are required for such occupation.

Not later than the relevant date, the tenant must have been

given written notice that possession might be required under this Case (formerly 1965 Act, s 15 or 1968 Act, Sched 3, Case 11).

(*f*) *Case 16: Former tied cottage.* The landlord requires premises at one time occupied by a person employed in agriculture under the terms of his employment (a tied cottage), for the occupation of a person whom he employs or will employ in agriculture.

A claim cannot succeed against a tenant whom the landlord formerly employed, nor against the widow of a former employee. The landlord must, not later than the relevant date, have given the tenant written notice that possession might be required under this Case (formerly 1965 Act, s 16 or 1968 Act, Sched 3, Case 12).

Neither this ground, nor either of the two following grounds, is available to recover possession of an agricultural tied cottage, where the tenancy would have been protected by the 1976 Act had the tenancy, or an earlier one granted to that tenant or a member of his family, been at a low rent.

(*g*) *Case 17: Farmhouse redundant on amalgamation.* The landlord requires premises affected by an amalgamation scheme approved under the Agriculture Act 1967, s 26, and put into effect, for a person employed or to be employed by him in agriculture.

When the proposals for the scheme were submitted, the premises must have been occupied by a person responsible for farming part of the land affected, whether as owner, tenant, servant or agent. The claim for possession cannot be effective against a person who was formerly so responsible for farming, nor a person at any time employed by the landlord in agriculture, nor the widow of either. The landlord must, before the start of the tenancy, have given the tenant written notice that possession might be required under this Case (formerly Agriculture Act 1967, s 38 or 1968 Act, Sched 3, Case 13). The possession proceedings must be begun within either five years after the approval of the amalgamation proposals, or three years after the premises first ceased to be occupied by a person formerly responsible for the farming (as above) or his widow.

This ground may not be available for a tied cottage (see above, para (*f*)).

(h) Case 18: Other former farmhouses. The landlord requires premises last occupied before the current tenancy by a person responsible, as owner, tenant, servant or agent, for farming land together with which the premises formed an agricultural unit (defined: Agriculture Act 1947, s 109 (2)) for the occupation either of a person who is or will be responsible for farming any of the land, or of a person whom he employs, or will employ, in agriculture.

The claim for possession cannot be effective against a person now or formerly so responsible for farming any of the land, or his widow, or against a present or former employee in agriculture. This ground does not apply if there was an amalgamation scheme under the Agriculture Act 1967, s 26, before the tenancy was granted. The landlord must, not later than the relevant date, have given the tenant notice that possession might be required under this Case (formerly 1968 Act, Sched 3, Case 14).

This ground may not be available for a tied cottage (see above, para *(f)*, p 26).

(i) Case 19: Protected shorthold tenancy. (See p 45).

(j) Case 20: Servicemen. The landlord was a member of the regular armed forces of the Crown when he acquired the premises and when he let them, and possession is required in one of the following circumstances (1980 Act, s 67, Sched 7):

(i) as a residence for the landlord;

(ii) if the landlord has died, in one of three cases: first, as a residence for a member of his family who resided with him when he died; secondly, as a residence for a successor in title who is not, and does not claim through, a purchaser for value; or thirdly, so that the premises may be sold with vacant possession;

(iii) a mortgagee, under a mortgage deed made before the mortgage was granted, is entitled to exercise a statutory or contractual power of sale, and requires to sell with vacant possession;

(iv) when the premises are not reasonably suitable to the landlord's needs having regard to his place of work, to use the proceeds of a sale with vacant possession to buy premises which are more suitable.

The tenancy must have been granted after s 67 of the 1980 Act came into force. Both in respect of the current tenancy, and of all earlier protected tenancies granted since then, the landlord must have given the tenant written notice, not later than the relevant date, that possession might be required under this Case. The court may dispense with these requirements as to notice if it is just and equitable to make an order for possession.

The regular armed forces of the Crown are: the Royal Navy; Her Majesty's military forces (excluding the army reserve, Territorial Army, forces raised under a colonial law, retired officers and officers on any reserve); Her Majesty's air forces (excluding the air force reserve, Royal Auxiliary Air Force, forces raised under a colonial law and retired officers); Queen Alexandra's Royal Naval Nursing Service; Women's Royal Naval Service (House of Commons Disqualification Act 1975, s 1).

(k) *Case 21: Overcrowding.* The premises are overcrowded in such circumstances as to render the occupier guilty of an offence (1977 Act, s 101).

In this case all protection of the control is removed from the tenant, so there is no question of the court going into all the circumstances. There are, however, exceptions:

    (i) if the tenant has applied to the local authority for suitable alternative accommodation (Housing Act 1957, s 78 (3)); or

    (ii) if the local authority had granted to the tenant a licence on the grounds of exceptional circumstances (Housing Act 1957, s 80).

The premises concerned in an application on this ground must be used or suitable for use as a separate dwelling by members of the working class.

(l) *Case 22: Unfit premises.* The premises are insanitary or unfit.

Where the owner has undertaken that premises shall not be used for human habitation, or a demolition or closing order has been made under the Housing Act 1957, or possession is required to enable a local authority to exercise any statutory housing powers (Housing Act 1957, ss 16 (5), 22 (5), 27 (5), 73 (4), 158 (1)). This applies even if the condition of the premises results from a breach of contractual or statutory duty by the landlord (*Buswell* v *Goodwin* [1971] 1 **WLR** 92).

(m) Case 23: New town purposes. The Secretary of State for the Environment certifies that possession is immediately required of premises acquired by a development corporation or a local highway authority for new town purposes (New Towns Act 1965, s 22 (3)).

(n) Case 24: Inadequate fire escape. The premises form part of a house in respect of which the owner has given an undertaking that it will not be used for human habitation because of inadequate means of escape from fire (1980 Act, Sched 24, para 9).

(o) Case 25: Extended tenancy. No tenant under an extended tenancy, granted under the Leasehold Reform Act 1967 to a tenant under a long lease at a low rent, has any right to security of tenure under the Rent Act, nor has any sub-tenant deriving title directly or indirectly under an extended tenancy (Leasehold Reform Act 1967, s 16 (1) *(d)*).

Chapter II
Regulated Tenancies: Registration of Rent

Statutes referred to in this chapter:
Rent Act 1977: '1977 Act.'
Housing Act 1980: '1980 Act.'

Forms referred to in this chapter are prescribed by:
Rent Regulation (Forms etc) Regulations 1978.

A — Rent to be Charged

1 Fair rent: the statutory formula

The rent which is to be registered is to be fixed, whether by the rent officer or a rent assessment committee, as a 'fair rent'. In assessing this, all the circumstances, and in particular the following, are to be taken into account (1977 Act, s 70 (1)):

    (a) the age of the premises;

    (b) the character of the premises;

    (c) the locality of the premises;

    (d) the state of repair of the premises; and

    (e) the quantity, quality and condition of any furniture provided for use under the tenancy.

Disrepair or other defects attributable to failure on the part of the tenant, or any predecessor in title of his, to comply with the terms of the regulated tenancy are to be ignored (1977 Act, s 70 (1) *(a)*). Conversely, improvements carried out by the tenant, or any predecessor in title of his, are also to be ignored unless the work was in compliance with an obligation under the tenancy (1977 Act, s 70 (1) *(b)*).

Where the regulated tenancy was converted from a controlled tenancy, these references to disrepair, defects and improvements extend to those occurring during the controlled tenancy (1977 Act, Sched 17, para 6). Improvements include the replacement of fixtures and fittings (1977 Act, s 70 (4)).

Where the registration relates to a statutory tenancy arising on the termination of a long tenancy at a low rent, it is to be assumed that the initial repairs have been completed (Leasehold Reform Act 1967, Sched 5, para 4 (4)).

Where furniture is provided, one must similarly ignore both improvements to it by the tenant or any predecessor in title, and any deterioration in its condition due to ill-treatment by the tenant, any person residing or lodging with him, or any subtenant (1977 Act, s 70 (3) *(e)*).

Scarcity value is also to be ignored. For this purpose the following statutory presumption must be made:

> 'that the number of persons seeking to become tenants of similar dwelling-houses in the locality on the terms (other than those relating to rent) of the regulated tenancy is not substantially greater than the number of such dwelling-houses in the locality which are available for letting on such terms' (1977 Act, s 80 (2)).

The locality, in this connection, should be a wide area (*Metropolitan Property Holdings Ltd* v *Finegold* [1975] 1 WLR 349 at p 353).

2 Fair rent: evidence for assessment

In fixing the fair rent, the greatest evidential weight is placed on 'comparables', other recent registrations of fair rents for similar properties in the same area (*Tormes Property Co Ltd* v *Landau* [1971] 1 QB 261; *Mason* v *Skilling* [1974] 1 WLR 1437). If there is no comparable from the same locality, one from a neighbouring district can be used (*Meredith* v *Stevens* (1974) 237 EG 573). A rent assessment committee may draw on its own knowledge and experience, even ignoring the evidence given (*Crofton Investment Trust* v *Greater London Rent Assessment Committee* [1967] 2 QB 955). The capital value of the premises can be used as a guide, but it is not conclusive. Exceptionally, the rent can be assessed as a percentage of the original capital cost, in which case no deduction should be made for scarcity value (*Anglo-Italian Properties* v *London Rent Assessment Panel* [1969] 1 WLR 730). A 10 per cent yield on the cost was used in that case and the cost of repairs added. When the calculation is based on capital value, the fact that the tenant is in possession is disregarded *(Mason v Skilling, supra)*.

Where services are concerned, actual figures are generally used, but can be reduced if considered excessive *(Metropolitan Properties Co Ltd v Noble* [1968] 1 WLR 838). If costs have increased between the date of the application and the date of the rent assessment committee's hearing, those increases can be taken into account *(Metropolitan Properites Co (FGC) Ltd v Lannon* [1968] 1 WLR 815, reversed on appeal on other grounds). Management charges can be included where incurred by the landlord in the provision of the services *(Metropolitan Properties Co Ltd v Noble, supra)*.

A corollary of the rule that the tenant's failure to repair must be ignored is that the landlord's failure to enforce the tenant's covenants must also be ignored *(Metropolitan Properties v Wooldridge* (1968) 20 P & CR 64). Where the premises have been seriously damaged, and that damage was not caused by the tenant's negligence or breach of the tenancy agreement, the fair rent is assessed on the basis of that damaged condition, and can therefore be nominal *(McGee v London Rent Assessment Panel* (1969) 113 SJ 384).

3 Rent to be registered

The sum to be entered on the register as the rent must be adjusted as follows:

> *(a)* It must include sums paid by the tenant to the landlord for the use of furniture or for services, even where dealt with separately, or under a separate agreement (1977 Act, s 71 (1)). The amount payable for services (unless variable under *(c)* below), if at least 5 per cent of the total, must be registered, and also the 'service element' for phasing purposes (1977 Act, Sched 8, para 2 (1));
>
> *(b)* It must exclude rates to be borne by the landlord or a superior landlord. A note is added to the register to show that the rates are payable in addition (1977 Act, s 71 (2);
>
> *(c)* It may be varied in accordance with contractual terms approved as reasonable which provide for adjustment in cases of variation of the cost to the landlord, or any superior

landlord, of the services provided for the tenant, or of works of maintenance or repair carried out (1977 Act, s 71 (4)).

. B — REGISTRATION APPLICATION BY LANDLORD AND/OR TENANT

The rent for a regulated tenancy is determined on an application for registration. Applications by the parties to the tenancy are dealt with in this section, and those by the local authority in the next one. The application is normally made during the currency of the tenancy. However, a landlord proposing to build or convert a house, or make improvements, may apply in advance for a determination of the rent, given as a 'certificate of fair rent', which will be registered after the work is completed. The same procedure is available for premises not at the time let for which no rent has been registered during the preceding two years (1977 Act, s 69 (4), Scheds 11, 12; 1980 Act, Sched 25, para 40).

An appeal from a rent assessment committee on a point of law only lies to the High Court (Tribunals and Inquiries Act 1971, s 13 (1)).

1 Representation

At oral consultations with the rent officer or hearings by the rent assessment committees the parties may be heard personally, or by any representative (1977 Act, Sched 11, paras 4 (3), 8, 12 (1), Sched 12, paras 4 (2), 7 (3)). Where the tenant is a serviceman on temporary service he may be represented by any person who satisfies the rent officer or the rent assessment committee that he is acting bona fide in the serviceman's interests, although it has not been possible to obtain the serviceman's instructions. Preliminary steps (eg, requesting an oral hearing) can also be taken by such a representative (Reserve and Auxiliary Force (Protection of Civil Interests) Act 1951, s 22 (1)–(3A); 1977 Act, Sched 23, para 9).

2 Subsisting regulated tenancies

The application for registration is made to the rent officer either by the landlord or by the tenant, or jointly by both. If the premises are let to a number of tenants jointly, all must apply (*Turley* v *Panton* (1975) 29 P & CR 397). The application is on Form No 5. The proposed rent must be stated (1977 Act, s 67 (2); *Chapman* v *Earl* [1968] 1 WLR 1315), or it must be calculable from what is said (*R* v *London Rent Assessment Panel, ex parte Braq Investments* [1969] 1 WLR 970). If the landlord applies, and the proposed rent includes a sum for services, that amount must be specified (1977 Act, s 67 (2); 1980 Act, s 59 (2)). The application form must then be accompanied by details of the landlord's expenditure in providing those services.

The procedure is the same whether the application is for a first registration or for the alteration of a rent already registered. Normally applications by one party alone cannot be made less than two years after the date when the last registration took effect, or the date of the last application for registration when the registered rent was confirmed unaltered (whichever was the later). The landlord may, however, apply within the last three months of that two years if the previous registration was made by a rent tribunal while the resident landlord control applied (1977 Act, Sched 2, para 6 (2)). If the local authority applies for the rent to be fixed, but the rent officer makes no registration, that does not count as confirmation for the purpose of the two-year rule (1977 Act, s 67 (3), (4); 1980 Act, s 60 (1)). The period is three years, rather than two years, if it runs from a date before s 60 of the 1980 Act came into force (1980 Act, s 60 (2)).

There is no restriction on an application if there is a change rendering the registered rent no longer fair. Once the rent officer decides there has been such a change, that decision cannot be challenged before the rent assessment committee (*London Housing and Commercial Properties Ltd* v *Cowan* [1977] 1 QB 178). The change must be in the condition of the premises (including improvements made to it, eg, the replacement of a boiler (ibid)), the terms of the tenancy, or any other circumstances taken into consideration when the rent was previously considered (1977 Act, s 67 (3)). Where the fair rent is reassessed during the two-year period, the change in the rent is not restricted to the alteration that made the re-assessment permissible, but must take account of all the factors then relevant.

On receipt of an application, the rent officer may by written notice. require the landlord or the tenant to give any further information that he reasonably requires and specifies in his notice, within a specified period (minimum seven days from the service of the notice). Such a notice can be served on a party whether or not he is the applicant (1977 Act, Sched 11, para 1). Except in the case of a joint application, the rent officer serves notice of the application on the other party to the tenancy, stating the rent specified in the application, what sum (if any) the landlord attributes to services, and giving a period of not less than seven days from the service of the notice for a request that he consider the rent in consultation with both parties (1977 Act, Sched 8, para 6, Sched 11, para 3; 1980 Act, Sched 6, para 2). If no such request is made, or if the application is a joint one, and if, considering the information supplied to him and any inquiry he thinks fit to make, the rent officer considers that the rent specified in the application is fair, he may proceed to register it. In that event he must notify the landlord and the tenant accordingly (1977 Act, Sched 11, paras 2, 3A; 1980 Act, Sched 6, para 2).

If there is to be a consultation, the rent officer appoints a time and place, and serves at least seven days' notice (14 days if details of expenditure on services have been supplied) of it on those concerned (1977 Act, Sched 11, para 4; 1980 Act, Sched 6, paras 3–5). The rent officer has power simultaneously to hold consultations in respect of the rent of more than one premises.

Having determined the rent after the consultation, or confirmed the rent already registered, the rent officer registers the new rent, or notes the confirmation on the register. He also notifies the landlord and the tenant. This notice must state that if either party serves written objection on the rent officer within twenty-eight days, or such longer period as he or a rent assessment committee may allow, the matter will be referred to such a committee (1977 Act, Sched 11, paras 5, 6). If the objection is out of time the rent officer may still refer it, or may seek a committee's directions as to whether to do so.

3 Appeals as to registration of rents

The rent assessment committee may by notice (on Form No 9) require landlord or tenant to give such further information as it reasonably requires, within a specified period of at least fourteen days. Failure to give this information is an offence. It must serve notice on both the landlord and the tenant giving at least fourteen days for making written representations or for requesting the opportunity to make oral representations (1977 Act, Sched 11, para 7). The landlord or the tenant who asks to make oral representations must be given an opportunity to be heard by the committee. Both parties are given at least ten days' notice of the date, time and place of the hearing (Rent Assessment Committees (England and Wales) Regulations 1971, reg 3 (3)). The committee must take all reasonable steps to supply each party before the hearing with copies or details of relevant documents received from the rent officer or the other party, or prepared by or for the committee for that appeal (reg 5).

The committee may decide to inspect the premises, and must do so, subject to obtaining any necessary consent, if either party requests it to (Rent Assessment Committees (England and Wales) Regulations 1971, reg 7 (1)). At a hearing, a party may give evidence, call witnesses and cross-examine the other party's witnesses. The committee determines the order in which it hears the parties (reg 4).

The committee's decision is either to confirm the rent officer's determination or to fix a different rent (1977 Act, Sched 11, para 9 (1)). The decision is recorded in writing, with reasons, but does not disclose whether it was unanimous or by a majority (Rent Assessment Committees (England and Wales) Regulations 1971, reg 10). In the absence of proper reasons, the Divisional Court may refer the decision back to the committee (*Guppy's Properties Ltd* v *Knott* (1979) 124 SJ 82). The committee notifies the rent officer of its decision, and he makes the appropriate entry in the register (1977 Act, Sched 11, para 9 (2), (3)).

Once an appeal has been lodged, it can only be withdrawn by agreement between the parties and with the sanction of the committee. That sanction may be withheld if the public interest so requires, eg, because a registered fair rent is used as a comparable in fixing other rents (*Hanson* v *Church Commissioners for England* [1978] QB 823).

4 Certificate of fair rent

A landlord proposing to build, convert or improve premises may apply on Form No 10 to the rent officer for a certificate of fair rent, assessed on the basis that a regulated tenancy is granted after the work is completed. The same procedure is available to the owner of property intending to let it. In this case the premises must not at the date of the application be subject to a regulated tenancy, and one of two conditions must be satisfied. Either no rent must be registered, or if one is it must have been registered or last confirmed more than two years before (1977 Act, s 69 (1); 1980 Act, Sched 25, para 40).

The issue of the certificate will, subject to certain conditions, enable the landlord to be sure that the rent specified in the certificate will become the registered rent when the work is completed or the tenancy granted. The application specifies the rent to be stated in the certificate and is accompanied by plans and specifications of the proposed work, where appropriate. It must state whether the premises are currently subject to a regulated tenancy. The proposed tenancy will be assumed to be on the terms stated in the application. If none is specified then the presumption is that the tenant will be liable only for internal decorative repairs, and that no services or furniture will be provided for him (1977 Act, s 69 (2)).

If the rent officer considers he has sufficient information, and that the rent stated in the application would be fair, he may issue a certificate accordingly, unless the premises are then subject to a regulated tenancy (1977 Act, Sched 12, paras 3–6). It could, of course, only be subject to such a tenancy where a conversion or improvement was proposed. If the rent officer is not satisfied, but considers he has sufficient information, he must serve a notice specifying a time, at least seven days after the service of his notice, and place where he will consider in consultation with the applicant (and the present tenant if it is proposed to improve premises then subject to a regulated tenancy) the rent to be specified in the certificate. The rent officer determines the fair rent and serves notice on the applicant (and the tenant if appropriate) that he will issue the certificate unless the applicant (or the tenant) requests that the application be referred to a rent assessment committee. The request must be made within fourteen days or such longer time as the rent officer or a rent assessment committee allows. If it is made late, the rent officer may still make the reference, or he may seek a committee's directions as to whether to do so. If no such request is made, the certificate is issued to the applicant (and the tenant).

If the rent officer considers that the application does not give him sufficient information to enable him to issue the certificate, he serves notice on the applicant saying that he will not entertain the application. The notice also states that if a written request is made to the rent officer within fourteen days from the service of the notice, or any longer period allowed by him or a rent assessment committee, he will refer the application to such a committee (1977 Act, Sched 12, para 2). If the request is out of time, the rent officer may still refer it, or seek a committee's directions as to whether to do so.

5 Appeals as to certificates of fair rent

A request for a certificate of fair rent may be referred to a rent assessment committee in either of two ways: on an appeal against the rent officer's determination of the fair rent, or on an appeal against his rejection of an application for lack of information.

On an appeal against a rejection for lack of information, if the committee also considers that the information is insufficient, it notifies the applicant accordingly (1977 Act, Sched 12, paras 7, 8). That is the end of the application; there is no provision for representations to be made.

On any other appeal, the procedure is as follows. The committee serves notice on the applicant (and the tenant, if the application is in respect of improvements to premises currently subject to a regulated tenancy) giving a period of at least fourteen days within which written representations, or a request to make oral representations, may be made. The period for asking to make oral representations may be extended by the committee. The party asking to make oral representations is afforded the opportunity of a hearing by the committee. Having heard the representations, the committee makes a determination and notifies the parties and the rent officer accordingly. The latter then issues a certificate to the applicant (and the tenant) specifying the rent determined by the committee.

6 Registration after issue of certificate of fair rent

The landlord or intending landlord can apply, on Form No 7, to the rent officer for registration of the rent of premises as specified in a certificate of fair rent within two years after the issue of the certificate (1977 Act, s 69 (4); 1980 Act, Sched 25, para 40). The rent officer must then ascertain whether the works specified in the certificate have been carried out (in the case of improvements or building works), or that the premises are in the same condition that they were in when the certificate was issued (where the application was made for unlet premises). If furniture is to be provided, he must be satisfied that its quantity, quality and condition accord with the particulars in the application for the certificate. If satisfied, he must register the rent in the certificate (1977 Act, Sched 11, para 10 (1), (2)). If he is not satisfied he must serve a notice on the applicant saying so. The notice must also state that if the applicant makes a written request to him within fourteen days, or such longer period as the rent officer or a rent assessment committee may allow, he will refer the matter to such a committee. If the request is out of time, the rent officer may still refer it, or may seek a committee's directions as to whether to do so.

The committee gives the applicant an opportunity to make written representations, or be heard orally, and then notifies the applicant whether or not it is satisfied. If it is satisfied, it directs the rent officer to register the rent specified in the certificate; otherwise it directs him to refuse the application for registration (1977 Act, Sched 11, para 12).

7 Failure to give information

It is an offence to fail without reasonable cause to give a rent assessment committee information specified in a notice from the committee requiring such information for the purposes of determining a fair rent. The penalty on summary conviction is a fine of up to £50 for the first offence, and up to £100 on subsequent convictions (1977 Act, Sched 11, para 7 (2), (3)). Where a body corporate commits the offence, any director, manager, secretary or similar officer of it, or person purporting to act in that capacity, with whose consent or connivance or by reason of whose neglect it was committed, is equally liable and punishable. The offence does not extend to failure to give information to a rent officer.

8 Cancellation of registration

The registration of a rent can be cancelled, and the register vacated, either on the joint application of the landlord and the tenant if the premises are then subject to a regulated tenancy, or, if they are not, on the sole application of the person who would be the landlord if they were (1977 Act, s 73 (1), (1A); 1980 Act, s 62 (2)).

Where there is no regulated tenancy, an application for cancellation can be made when two years have elapsed since the registration became effective. When a regulated tenancy is subsisting, the parties must enter into a rent agreement taking effect at least two years from the effective date of the last registration (1980 Act, Sched 25, para 40). That agreement either increases the rent payable, or it grants a new tenancy at a higher rent. Its terms must be such that the tenancy does not end, and cannot be brought to an end by the landlord (except for non-payment of rent or breach of the terms of the tenancy), earlier than twelve months after the date of the application to the rent officer. The agreement may be conditional on the application for cancellation being successful.

A joint application is made to the rent officer on Form No 8, accompanied by a copy of the rent agreement (Rent Regulation (Cancellation of Registration of Rent) Regulations 1972).

The rent officer may serve notice on either party requiring further information to be given to him within not less than seven days. The rent officer must be satisfied that the rent payable under the rent agreement, or the highest rent so payable, does not exceed the fair rent, and that any terms for the payment of varying sums for services, maintenance or repairs are reasonable. If not satisfied by the application and any further information supplied to him, the rent officer must serve notice on the landlord and tenant that he proposes to hold a consultation. If satisfied, the rent officer must cancel the registration. In any event, he must notify the applicants of his decision. The cancellation cannot take effect until the rent agreement starts.

Regulations have not yet been made governing the procedure on an application for cancellation where there is no subsisting tenancy.

Even though a registration has been cancelled, a fresh application to register a fair rent can always be made.

C — REGISTRATION APPLICATION BY LOCAL AUTHORITY

A local authority (here meaning the council of a district or London borough, the Common Council of the City of London and the Council of the Isles of Scilly) may apply to the rent officer for the consideration of the fair rent of any premises in their area for which a rent may be or has been registered (1977 Act, s 68; 1980 Act, Sched 25, para 40). Where a fair rent has already been registered, a local authority may not apply within two years of that registration, unless some circumstances taken into consideration when the rent was last registered have changed so as to render the registered rent no longer fair. Examples of circumstances that may be changed are: the condition of the premises, including the making of any improvements, and the terms of the tenancy.

By analogy with local authorities' powers in cases under the rent tribunal's jurisdiction, it is likely that they are entitled to make block applications to the rent officer, comprising a number of tenancies. They would have to have given consideration to each individual one, but would not need to obtain the tenants' consent (*R* v *Barnet and Camden Rent Tribunal, ex parte Frey Investments Ltd* [1972] 2 QB 342).

On an application by a local authority the rent officer may seek further information from the landlord or the tenant, and must serve notice on them giving at least seven days for written representations as to whether a rent should be registered, and if so what rent (Rent Regulation (Local Authority Applications) Regulations 1972). If the rent payable does not in the rent officer's view exceed the fair rent, he takes no action as a result of the local authority's application.

If, on the other hand, he thinks the contractual rent, or the highest contractual rent, exceeds the fair rent he must invite the landlord and the tenant (but not the local authority) to a consultation, and subsequently register a fair rent. Either party may appeal to the rent assessment committee.

Chapter III
Protected Shorthold Tenancies

Statute referred to in this chapter:
Housing Act 1980: '1980 Act.'

Protected shorthold tenancies are a type of regulated tenancy. It is convenient to consider this as a separate control because of the detailed requirements that a tenancy must satisfy to fall within it, and the important consequences for security of tenure.

A — EXTENT OF CONTROL

This control applies if the answer to the following five questions is Yes.

(1) *Was the tenancy granted after s 52 of the 1980 Act came into force and to a tenant who was not immediately beforehand a protected or statutory tenant of those premises?* (1980 Act, s 52 (1), (2))

Section 52 must be brought into force by a commencement order (1980 Act, s 153 (4)).

(2) *Was the tenancy granted for a term certain of at least one year, but not more than five years?* (1980 Act, s 52 (1), (5))

The landlord must not have power to terminate the tenancy prematurely, except under a provision for re-entry or forfeiture on non-payment of rent or breach of any other term of the agreement. A tenancy for a term certain and thereafter periodically, or one capable of extension at the tenant's option, is a protected shorthold tenancy for the initial fixed term.

(3) *Before the tenancy was granted, did the landlord give the tenant notice, complying with prescribed requirements, that the tenancy was to be protected shorthold tenancy?* (1980 Act, s 52 (1) *(b)*, (3))

(4) *Was a rent registered when the tenancy was granted, or had*

a certificate of fair rent already been issued? (1980 Act, s 52
(1) *(c)*)

If no rent is registered, two conditions must be fulfilled. First,
an application to register the rent must be made within 28 days
of the grant of the tenancy, and not withdrawn. Secondly, until
the rent is registered, the rent charged must be limited to the
amount specified in the certificate of fair rent.

(5) *In other respects, does the tenancy qualify as a regulated
tenancy (pp 1–7)?*

B — RENT TO BE CHARGED

When a protected shorthold tenancy begins, a rent must be
registered, or an application made to register one. While the
application is pending, a certificate of fair rent must be in force
and the landlord must not charge any more rent than the figure
given in the certificate. Apart from that, there are no special
rules as to the rent to be charged. Those that govern regulated
tenancies apply to protected shorthold tenancies.

C— SECURITY OF TENURE

1 End of fixed term

When the fixed term of a protected shorthold tenancy comes
to an end, the tenancy continues unless either party takes steps
to bring it to an end. If the agreement for the tenancy provides
for it to continue on a yearly or other basis, it is a protected
tenancy. Otherwise, a statutory tenancy arises. Although once
the fixed term ends the tenancy is no longer a protected shorthold tenancy, the landlord's power to obtain possession is not
prejudiced.

2 Termination by tenant

Even though a protected shorthold tenancy must be granted
for a fixed term, the tenant has the right to end it during that
fixed term by notice (1980 Act, s 53). An agreement purporting
to impose a penalty or disability on a tenant who exercises that
right is void. The length of notice that a tenant must give
depends on the length of the tenancy granted by the landlord, as
follows:

Length of tenancy term	*Minimum notice by tenant*
Two years or less	One month
Over two years	Three months

3 Sub-tenants

Most sub-tenancies granted out of protected shorthold tenancies do not give the sub-tenant security of tenure against the head landlord (1980 Act, s 54 (1)). Once the head landlord is entitled to possession against the protected shorthold tenant, he is also entitled to possession against the sub-tenant.

This applies to sub-tenancies created at any time during a specified continuous period (1980 Act, s 54 (3)). It runs from the grant of the protected shorthold tenancy until a protected tenancy of the premises is granted to someone who immediately beforehand was not a protected or statutory tenant, or until there is no such tenant in possession.

D — GROUNDS FOR POSSESSION

All the grounds for possession that relate to regulated tenancies can apply to protected shorthold tenancies. In addition, there is a special mandatory ground, Case 19 (1980 Act, s 55). The landlord is entitled to possession if the answer to the following two questions is Yes:

(1) *Is the tenancy a protected shorthold tenancy, or since it ended have tenancies only been granted to someone who immediately beforehand was a protected or statutory tenant?*

The court may waive strict compliance with the conditions for a protected shorthold tenancy. It can make a possession order notwithstanding the lack of preliminary notice to the tenant, or the lack of a registered rent or a certificate of fair rent linked to an application for registration and a rent limited to the certificate figure in the meantime. The court exercises this jurisdiction if it is just and equitable to do.

(2) *Did the landlord give the tenant at least three months' notice, and take proceedings within three months of the expiry of that notice?*

The notice has to be in writing and state that proceedings

may be brought under Case 19. The times for serving it are: the last three months of the fixed term tenancy, the three months preceding any anniversary of its expiry, or not earlier than a periodic tenancy could then be brought to an end by notice to quit served by the landlord. If one notice is allowed to expire without proceedings being taken, three months must elapse from its expiry before a new one is served.

Chapter IV
Lettings by Resident Landlords

Statutes referred to in this chapter:
Rent Act 1977: '1977 Act.'
Housing Act 1980: '1980 Act.'

Rent tribunals, under whose jurisdiction this control operates, have been abolished as separate entities (1980 Act, s 72). Their functions are now performed by rent assessment committees, using the name 'rent tribunal'.

A — EXTENT OF CONTROL

This control, making the tenancies into restricted contracts, applies if the answer to the following six questions is Yes (1977 Act, ss 12, 20; 1980 Act, s 65 (1)):

(1) *Are the premises a dwelling-house let in circumstances which, if this control did not apply, would give rise to a regulated tenancy?*

This control confers a privileged position on resident landlords who qualify, in cases which would otherwise be regulated tenancies. The conditions for a regulated tenancy – eg, that the premises are a dwelling-house, that the letting is a true tenancy, that the landlord is not exempt, etc – must therefore be considered.

(2) *Do the premises form part only of a building, which, unless the premises are part only of a flat, is not itself a purpose-built block of flats?*

A purpose-built block of flats is a building that as constructed contained, and still contains, two or more flats. A flat is defined as a dwelling-house separated horizontally from another dwelling-house forming part of the same building (1977 Act, Sched 2, para 4).

(3) *Did the landlord, when he granted the tenancy, occupy as*

his residence another dwelling-house in the same building as the premises?

Occupation as a residence is judged for this purpose by the criteria applied to a statutory tenant (1977 Act, Sched 2, para 5). An extension, which a landlord occupied, physically tied to the house but without intercommunication, was held not to be in the same building for this purpose (*Bardrick* v *Haycock* (1976) 31 P & CR 420).

For a furnished letting granted before 14 August 1974, the occupation on that date of the landlord, or, if the landlord's interest was vested in trustees as such, of a beneficiary for whom that interest or the proceeds of sale of it were held, suffices (1977 Act, Sched 24, para 6). Similarly, this condition is satisfied if on 14 August 1974 the landlord's interest was vested in personal representatives, in the Probate Judge under the Administration of Estates Act 1925, s 9, or in trustees as such, and the residence qualification was satisfied by the deceased immediately before his death, or by the settlor immediately before the creation of the settlement.

(4) *At all times since the tenancy was granted, has another dwelling-house in the same building as the premises or, as the case may be, another part of the same flat, been occupied as a residence by either —*

    (a) the landlord for the time being, or

    (b) a beneficiary for whom the landlord's interest, or the proceeds of sale of it, are held by trustees in whom it is vested? (1977 Act, s 12 (1) *(c)*, Sched 2, para 2)

In determining whether the landlord has been resident continuously, the following periods of absence may be disregarded (1977 Act, Sched 2, para 1; 1980 Act, s 65 (3)):

    (i) up to 28 days from the date when the landlord's interest at law and in equity became vested in a non-resident individual;

    (ii) up to six months from the date of such vesting, if during the first 28 days the landlord gave the tenant written notice of his intention to become resident in the building. The period to be disregarded ends if the landlord's interest changes hands again, or the landlord becomes resident;

(iii) up to two years during which the landlord's interest is vested in:

    (a) a deceased's personal representative, acting as such;

    (b) trustees as such;

    (c) the Probate Judge under the Administration of Estates Act 1925, s 9.

(5) *If let unfurnished, was the tenancy granted on or after 14 August 1974?*

(6) *If, immediately before the grant of this tenancy, the tenant was tenant of the premises or some other dwelling-house in the building, was that former tenancy outside the classes of protected and statutory tenancy?* (1977 Act, s 12 (2); 1980 Act, s 69 (4))

B — Rent to be Charged

Until a rent has been determined by a rent tribunal, there is no limit to the rent that can be charged on a new letting. When a rent tribunal determines a rent, it is registered in the register maintained by the president of the rent assessment panel (1977 Act, ss 78, 79; 1980 Act, Sched 25, para 43).

1 Determination of rent

The landlord, the tenant or the local authority (even without the tenant's consent: *R* v *Barnet and Camden Rent Tribunal, ex parte Frey Investments Ltd* [1972] 2 QB 342) can refer a letting to the rent tribunal at any time while it is subsisting, even if notice to quit determining it has already been served. Where there are joint tenants, all must join in the application (*Turley* v *Panton* (1975) 29 P & CR 397). An application cannot be withdrawn after the tribunal has entered upon consideration of it (see *R* v *Tottenham District Rent Tribunal, ex parte Fryer Bros (Properties) Ltd* [1971] 2 QB 681). The tribunal may by written notice require the landlord to give particulars of the tenancy. This he must do within the time stated in the notice, which must be at least seven days. Failure to give information is an offence. On summary conviction a landlord is liable to a fine of up to £50 for the first offence, and up to £100 thereafter (1977 Act, s 77).

There is no statutory guidance to rent tribunals on the princi-

ples to be adopted in determining rents, except that they may
not reduce a rent below what would be payable as a fair rent for
those premises. They have power to consider all the circumstances and fix such rent as they think reasonable, for a limited
period only if they wish. They take into account the services
actually provided by the landlord, even if these exceed those he
is contractually bound to provide. The tribunal can either
increase or decrease the rent, or may merely confirm it (1977
Act, s 78).

The amount of rent registered is exclusive of rates, but if the
rates are paid by the landlord or a superior lessor, that fact is
noted on the register. Registrations before 14 August 1974
may have been of a rent inclusive of rates. If there is still such an
entry on the register, the landlord cannot recover rates in
addition to the registered rent (*Dominal Securities Ltd* v *McLead*
(1978) 122 SJ 644).

There is an appeal within 28 days from a decision of a rent
tribunal on a point of law to the Divisional Court of the Queen's
Bench Division, or a party may require the tribunal to state a
case for the opinion of the court (Tribunals and Inquiries Act
1971, s 13 (1)). Prerogative orders will also issue against rent tribunals in appropriate cases.

The amount of rent registered is exclusive of rates, but if the
rates are paid by the landlord or a superior lessor, that fact is
noted on the register.

2 Varying a registered rent

Normally a rent tribunal is not required to entertain a reference to consider a rent until two years have expired since that
rent was last considered, unless the application is made jointly
by landlord and tenant (1977 Act, s 80 (2); 1980 Act, s 70). The
two-year period is extended to three years for rents registered
before s 70 of the 1980 Act came into force.

Exceptionally, there may be an earlier reconsideration on the
ground of a change in the condition of the premises, the furniture or services provided, or the terms of the tenancy or other
circumstances taken into consideration when the rent was last
considered. The change must be such as to make the registered
rent no longer reasonable. A rent may only be reconsidered

when there is a subsisting letting (*R* v *East London Rent Tribunal, ex parte Schryer* [1970] 1 QB 686).

3 Excess rent

Once a rent has been registered, it is unlawful to require or receive payment of a greater sum (1977 Act, s 81). Any excess paid is recoverable by the payer. Furthermore, the landlord who requires or receives any excess commits an offence. He is liable on summary conviction to a fine of up to £100, imprisonment for up to six months, or both. The convicting court can order repayment to the tenant of the excess paid, without prejudice to any other method of recovery. A tenant who knows of the limit and offers more than the registered rent may also commit an offence, in aiding and abetting, or inciting, the landlord to commit an offence.

C — SECURITY OF TENURE

The 1980 Act introduced entirely new provisions as to security of tenure for tenants under this control. The new rules only apply, however, to lettings granted on or after the date that s 69 of the 1980 Act came into force (1977 Act, s 102A; 1980 Act, s 69 (3)). The previous rules continue to apply to earlier lettings.

1 Post-1980 Act lettings

The only security of tenure that tenants enjoy is the power of the court to stay or suspend the execution of a possession order, or to postpone the date for possession for up to three months (1977 Act, s 106A; 1980 Act, s 69 (2)). When exercising this power, the court must impose conditions as to payment of the current rent and any arrears, unless to do so would cause the tenant exceptional hardship or otherwise be unreasonable. This delaying power can be exercised in favour of a tenant's spouse occupying the premises under the Matrimonial Homes Act 1967.

The limitation on the tenant's security of tenure can continue to apply for a limited period after the landlord's death, even though there is then no resident landlord. If the landlord died after s 65 of the 1980 Act came into force, the position remains the same while the reversion is vested in the landlord's personal representatives acting in that capacity, for a maximum period of two years (1977 Act, Sched 2, para 2A; 1980 Act, s 65 (5), (7)).

2 Pre-1980 Act lettings

Security of tenure operates by the rent tribunal postponing the operation of a notice to quit. There is no provision for security for a tenant whose tenancy expires by effluxion of time. Security may be obtained in two ways: upon a reference to the tribunal to consider or reconsider the rent, and upon an application for security. It may not be available where the landlord formerly occupied the premises.

(a) On consideration of rent

When a landlord serves a notice to quit after the contract has been referred to the tribunal by the tenant or the local authority, but either before the tribunal gives its decision or within six months thereafter, it does not take effect until the expiration of the six months, unless the tribunal directs that a shorter time be substituted (1977 Act, s 103). The period of security is therefore automatically six months unless the tribunal otherwise directs. If the reference to the tribunal is withdrawn, the notice is suspended until seven days from the withdrawal.

(b) On application for security

An application specifically for security may be made to the rent tribunal under s 104 of the 1977 Act, whenever a tenancy has been referred to a tribunal by any of the parties, and a notice to quit has been served. Unlimited successive applications for security may be made before the notice (as in effect extended) expires. Subject to the limitations in the next paragraph, the rent tribunal may each time suspend the operation of the notice by any period up to six months from the date when it would otherwise have taken effect. If it refuses an application for an extension, the notice does not take effect before seven days after the determination of the application.

(c) Tenant's misbehaviour

Application may be made to the rent tribunal for a direction that the period of suspension be reduced, which if granted also prevents the tenant from obtaining any further period of suspension (1977 Act, s 106).

The grounds upon which a direction may be made are:

(a) that the tenant has not complied with the terms of tenancy;

(b) that the tenant or any person residing or lodging with him has been guilty of conduct which is a nuisance or annoyance to adjoining occupiers;

(c) that the tenant or any person residing or lodging with him has been convicted of using the premises or allowing them to be used for an immoral or illegal purpose:

(d) that the condition of the premises has deteriorated owing to any act or neglect of the tenant or any person residing or lodging with him. This ground may apply notwithstanding that the landlord has failed to comply with his repairing obligations under the Housing Act 1961 (*Campbell* v *Daramola* (1974) 235 EG 687);

(e) that the condition of any furniture provided for the tenant's use has deteriorated owing to ill-treatment by the tenant or any person residing or lodging with him.

3 No resident landlord

Special provisions apply during any period during which there is no resident landlord, but which may be disregarded in determining whether this control applies. During such a period, an order for possession may only be made if one of the grounds justifying an order for possession of premises let on a regulated tenancy applies (1977 Act, Sched 3, para 3). If that period comes to an end, but without another landlord becoming resident, the tenancy becomes a regulated statutory tenancy (*Landau* v *Sloane* [1980] 3 WLR 197).

Chapter V
Other Restricted Contracts

Statutes referred to in this chapter:
Rent Act 1977: '1977 Act.'
Housing Act 1980: '1980 Act.'

A — EXTENT OF CONTROL

The scope of the jurisdiction of rent tribunals (now exercised by rent assessment committees: 1980 Act, s 72) over lettings, other than those by resident landlords, was greatly reduced in 1974. Although furnished lettings are now regulated, there are still cases within this control, eg, premises held under a licence (*R* v *South Middlesex Rent Tribunal, ex parte Beswick* (1976) 32 P & CR 67). In this context, 'tenant' and 'letting' are used with the appropriate extended meanings.

Premises will come within this control if the answer to the following six questions is Yes.

(1) *Is the tenant entitled to occupy all or part of a house as a residence?*

The residential requirement excludes intentionally temporary lettings, such as of hotel rooms (*R* v *Rent Tribunals for Bethnal Green and Paddington, ex parte Rowton Houses Ltd* (1947) 91 SJ 225), and also precludes corporations from claiming protection. The right to occupy for a holiday is specifically excluded from the control (1977 Act, s 19 (7)). A rent tribunal accepted jurisdiction in the case of a caravan used as a permanent dwelling ((1972) 227 EG 515).

(2) *Does the tenant pay a rent which includes a payment for the use of furniture or for services?* (1977 Act, s 19 (2))

No specified amount or proportion of furniture or services has to be provided by the landlord, but the *de minimis* rule applies to exclude very small amounts from consideration. 'Furniture' is construed according to its contemporary popular meaning. An article can be included in the definition although in law it is a fixture, but not if at the date of the contract it constituted part of the dwelling-house. 'Services' is defined to include attendance, the provision of heating and lighting and the supply of hot water. It extends to any other privilege or facility connected with the occupancy, except one requisite for the purposes of access, cold water supply or sanitary accommodation (1977 Act, s 19 (8)). Services can therefore include facilities outside the premises let, eg, use of the garden. The definition must be read subject to the limitation that the tenant must be contractually entitled to the services. (Other services may be taken into account in determining the rent, but do not count when considering whether the control applies at all.)

(3) *Do the terms of the letting exclude it from being a regulated tenancy or a housing association tenancy and from the control relating to agricultural tied cottages?* (1977 Act, s 19 (5) (a), (d), (e)).

(4) *Is the rateable value of the premises within any of the following limits?* (1977 Act, s 19 (4))

Rateable value on	Premises in Greater London	Elsewhere
23 March 1965	£400	£200
1 April 1973	£1,500	£750

For premises first entered in the valuation list after 23 March 1965, substitute the date of that entry for the next earlier date in the table.

If the premises are not separately rated, the rent tribunal has jurisdiction if it considers that it would have were the rateable value to be apportioned. The only exception to this is when in the course of proceedings the landlord requires an apportionment to be made, and within two weeks he brings proceedings in the county court for the making of such an apportionment (1977 Act, s 82).

(5) *Is none, or no substantial part, of the rent attributable to board?* (1977 Act, s 19 (5) (c))

What must be considered is the value to the tenant of the amount attributable to board.

(6) *Is the landlord someone other than one of the authorities listed below?* (1977 Act, s 19 (5) *(aa), (b)*; 1980 Act, s 73 (2), Sched 25, para 36)

The landlords whose lettings are excluded from this control are:

> *(a)* The Crown, unless the premises are managed by the Crown Estate Commissioners, a government department and trustees holding for any of them;

> *(b)* A local authority, ie, a county, district or London borough council, the Greater London Council, the Common Council of the City of London and the Council of the Isles of Scilly;

> *(c)* The Commission for the New Towns or a new town development corporation;

> *(d)* The Development Board for Rural Wales.

B — Rent to be Charged

The rules governing the rent that may be charged under a restricted contract are set out in Chapter IV.

C — Security of Tenure

A landlord seeking possession of premises let under a restricted contract that is a licence must do so only by taking legal proceedings, as in the case of a tenancy, if the contract in question was granted after s 69 of the 1980 Act came into force (Protection from Eviction Act 1977, s 3 (2A); 1980 Act, s 69 (1)). The rules conferring security of tenure are the same as on lettings by a resident landlord (Chapter IV). The same distinction must be drawn between lettings before the 1980 Act provisions came into force, and those made later. There is an additional curb on the tribunal's powers in pre-1980 Act cases. The operation of a notice to quit cannot be suspended by a rent tribunal if (1977 Act, s 105):

> *(a)* the landlord formerly occupied the premises as his residence;

(b) the landlord does not reside in any other part of the same house;

(c) when the notice to quit takes effect the premises are required as a residence for the former owner-occupier or any member of his family who resided with him when he last occupied them as his residence; and

(d) the tenant was given written notice on or before the granting of the tenancy that the landlord was owner-occupier within the meaning of the 1977 Act, s 105 (formerly Rent Act 1965, s 40 or Rent Act 1968, s 79). In the case of a letting subsisting on 8 December 1965, notice must have been given before 8 June 1966.

Chapter VI
Shared Accommodation

Statute referred to in this chapter:
Rent Act 1977: '1977 Act.'

A — EXTENT OF CONTROL

Although the controls in this chapter are those that apply where accommodation is shared, the tenant must also be entitled to exclusive occupation of some premises for any form of control to apply. The rateable value of those separately occupied premises must be within the limits for protected tenancies. Once some exclusive occupation is established, two questions need to be asked:

(1) *Is the accommodation that is shared living accommodation?*

(2) *If so, with whom does the tenant share?*

If the accommodation shared comes within the category of living accommodation, of which a definition has been attempted by the courts, the controls applied are those dealt with in this Chapter. If the accommodation shared is outside the category, the tenancy can be regulated in an appropriate case: the sharing does not then affect the position.

'Living accommodation' cannot be precisely defined. It seems to include those rooms which any member of the household uses for a considerable part of the day, rather than just visiting them, so that sharing must necessarily lead to an invasion of privacy. A kitchen and a sitting room are normally within the definition; a bathroom, WC, coal-house and garage are not.

B — SHARING WITH LANDLORD
(WITH OR WITHOUT OTHERS)

Where a tenant has exclusive occupation of some accommodation, but under the terms of his tenancy shares living accommodation with his landlord, either alone or with others as well, the letting is a restricted contract. This is the case where there would be a regulated tenancy, were it not for that sharing, and, if applicable, the operation of the resident landlord control (1977 Act, s 21). The rent fixing and security of tenure provisions governing lettings by a resident landlord (Chapter IV) therefore apply here.

If the accommodation was originally shared with another tenant, but he bought the reversion and so became the landlord, this is the control that now applies. The date when the position must be ascertained is the date of bringing an action (*Birch* v *Heasman* [1950] CLY 3428).

C — SHARING WITH PERSONS OTHER THAN LANDLORD OR SUB-TENANT

Where a tenant under the terms of his tenancy shares living accommodation with one or more persons other than his landlord, the accommodation in respect of which he is entitled to exclusive possession is deemed to be premises let on a protected tenancy (1977 Act, s 22 (1)).

1 Rent to be charged

The provisions for determining the rent under a regulated or a controlled tenancy, as the case may be, apply.

2 Security of tenure

A distinction must be drawn here between the separate accommodation, of which the tenant is entitled to exclusive possession, and the shared accommodation. The separate accommodation is expressly governed by the provisions governing protected tenancies. In effect the position of the shared accommodation is the same (subject to what is said in the next paragraph). No order can be made for possession of the shared accommodation, unless a similar order relating to the separate accommodation is made at the same time or has previously been made (1977 Act, s 22 (5)).

Where the tenancy contains a term that the landlord can terminate or modify the tenant's rights over the shared accommodation, certain modifications can be made, although these powers are subject to statutory restriction. A contractual right is, however, essential before the Act's provisions can be brought into operation. For this purpose, different rules apply according to whether or not the premises shared constitute living accommodation.

(a) Living accommodation shared — The landlord cannot terminate or modify the tenant's rights over shared living accommodation (eg, times when a kitchen may be used), except, where the contractual terms so provide, by varying or increasing the number of people entitled to use the accommodation (1977 Act, s 22 (3), (4)). The county court, on the landlord's application, may order any modification that it thinks just, but it has no power to terminate such rights (1977 Act, s 22 (6)).

(b) Other accommodation shared — The landlord's contractual powers to terminate or modify a tenant's rights over shared accommodation outside the definition of living accommodation are unrestricted. The county court's powers in respect of this accommodation extend to terminating the tenant's rights as well as modifying them (1977 Act, s 22 (6)).

D — SHARING WITH SUB-TENANT

The tenant of accommodation subject to a protected tenancy who sub-lets part only of the premises on terms that he shares living accommodation with his sub-tenant does not thereby lose his rights against the landlord or any superior landlord (1977 Act, s 23). If, as is unlikely, the sub-letting is one of the terms on which the landlord let to the tenant, the previous section will apply as far as necessary. The position of the sub-tenant against the tenant is of course that of a tenant sharing with his landlord, and the rules set out in the section dealing with that situation apply.

Chapter VII
Long Tenancies

Statutes referred to in this chapter:
Landlord and Tenant Act 1954: '1954 Act.'
Leasehold Reform Act 1967: '1967 Act.'
Rent Act 1977: '1977 Act.'

A — EXTENT OF CONTROL

This control is imposed by Pt I of the 1954 Act. Its effect is to continue a long tenancy automatically and indefinitely until the Act's procedure is put into effect. The tenant is then granted a statutory regulated tenancy (1954 Act, s 1). The parties to a lease may not contract out of this control (1954 Act, s 17), so an option which could result in the premature determination of such a lease, and the landlord obtaining vacant possession, is void (*Re Hennessey's Agreement* [1975] 2 Ch 252).

Minor amendments to the 1954 Act and the 1967 Act, replacing references to repealed Acts, are not given, as they do not affect the substance of the statutes.

For the control to apply, the answer to the following two questions must be Yes:

(1) *Was the tenancy originally granted for over twenty-one years at a rent less than two-thirds of the rateable value?*
(1954 Act, ss 1, 2; 1977 Act, Sched 23, paras 12, 13)

The control applies even if the original tenancy of over twenty-one years has subsequently been extended by statute or agreement between the parties, possibly for a shorter period (1954 Act, s 2 (4)).

In comparing the rent with the rateable value, sums which merely reimburse the landlord are ignored. These sums are any part of the rent expressed to be payable in respect of rates, services, repairs, maintenance or insurance, unless the parties could not have regarded it as so payable.

The rateable value to be used for comparison is, with one

61

exception, that on 23 March 1965, or the first day thereafter that the premises appeared on the valuation list (1977 Act, s 25 (3)). The exception comprises those properties first rated on or before 22 March 1973 whose rateable values then exceeded £400 in Greater London or £200 elsewhere. In that case, the comparison is with the rateable value on 22 March 1973

(2) *Would the tenancy be regulated if the letting had not been at a rent less than two-thirds of their rateable value?*

B — RENT TO BE CHARGED

Unless and until the steps outlined in the next section are taken to grant a statutory tenancy to the tenant, the original long tenancy is continued (1954 Act, s 3 (1)). If the whole of the premises are such that the tenancy would otherwise be regulated, the rent remains unaltered. If only part of the premises so qualifies, this control only applies to that part and the rent formerly payable is apportioned (1954 Act, s 3 (2), (3)). If an apportionment of the rent cannot be agreed between the parties, either may apply to the county court (1954 Act, s 3 (4)).

1 Amount of rent

The rent registration provisions applicable to regulated tenancies apply to fixing the rent. An application can be made to the rent officer to fix the fair rent even before the long tenancy comes to an end, but not before the other terms of the statutory tenancy have been agreed (1967 Act, Sched 5, para 4 (2)).

2 Initial repairs

The landlord will have to make an application to the court to determine the terms of the statutory tenancy. In that application he may state that he is willing to carry out certain repairs at the beginning of the tenancy. The tenant also may agree to carry out initial repairs. The court may order either party to carry out the repairs so specified by them, subject to the limitation that the repairs do not go beyond those necessary to put the premises in 'good repair'. This standard is defined as including both structure and decoration, having regard to the age, character and locality of the house (1954 Act, s 9). The incentive to the landlord to carry out repairs is that the rent will be determined according to the state of the premises when they have been done. If the need for the repairs stems from the tenant's breach of his obligations under the long tenancy, the landlord can recover their cost, either as a lump sum or by instalments (1954 Act, s 8).

If the landlord fails within a reasonable time to carry out the initial repairs which were his responsibility, the tenant can apply to the county court for an order reducing the rent (1954 Act, Sched 2, paras 1–3). If the tenant fails to do initial repairs which were his responsibility, or if he fails to pay any sum due to the landlord for repairs arising from his previous default, this is treated as a breach of an obligation under the tenancy and is a ground for the landlord obtaining possession (1954 Act, Sched 2, para 4; Sched 1, para 17).

C — SECURITY OF TENURE

1 Procedure

As already stated, a long tenancy to which this control applies continues unless determined in accordance with the provisions of the 1954 Act. The tenant may bring it to an end by at least one month's written notice to his immediate landlord to take effect at or after the contractual termination date of the original term (1954 Act, s 5). The landlord (a term specially defined: see below) may bring it to an end by serving notice in the prescribed form on the tenant (1954 Act, s 4).

The landlord's notice specifies the date on which the tenancy is to come to an end. This may be the contractual termination date, or later, and must be more than six but less than twelve months after the date of service of the notice. The notice must also specify the premises believed to qualify for protection. Either it must state that the landlord proposes to apply to the court for possession on one or more of the grounds specified in the next section, or it must contain proposals for a statutory tenancy should the tenant be unwilling to give up possession. The proposals must include the following:

(a) The amount of rent, when payable, and whether in advance or arrear;

(b) what initial repairs are to be carried out, which by the landlord and which by the tenant, and which are the tenant's responsibility because of prior breaches of covenant and how these are to be paid for; and

(c) what repairing obligations (if any) there are to be during the statutory tenancy, apart from the execution of initial repairs (1954 Act, ss 4 (3), 7 (2), 8 (4)).

The landlord's notice to resume possession must require the tenant to notify the landlord in writing within two months whether he is willing to give up possession. If the terms of the statutory tenancy have not been agreed by two months before the date of expiry given in the landlord's notice proposing the terms, his notice is ineffective unless he applies to the county court (1954 Act, s 7 (2)). The application must be made while the notice is current, and not earlier than two months after it was given (or one month if the tenant elects to retain possession) (1954 Act, s 7 (5)). A landlord who has served notice to resume possession may apply to the county court for possession on the ground specified in his notice, either within two months after the tenant elects to retain possession, or if he does not do so, at least two but not more than four months after the service of the notice (1954 Act, s 13 (1)).

2 'The landlord'

For the purposes of serving notices under the 1954 Act, and the provisions relating to initial repairs, the landlord is specially defined. He must be a person with a reversion expectant on the termination of the tenancy who is entitled to either the fee simple or a tenancy with at least five years longer to run than the protected tenancy. If the immediate landlord does not qualify, the next one who does up the chain leading to the freeholder fulfils the statutory definition. The only exceptions are the Crown, except where the premises are managed by the Crown Estate Commissioners, and government departments, to whom these provisions do not apply. If one of these would otherwise be the landlord for the purposes of the Act, then their immediate tenant takes on the role (1954 Act, s 21).

D — GROUNDS FOR POSSESSION

1 Before statutory tenancy starts

The landlord may apply to the county court for possession of property comprised in a long tenancy to which this control applies, after the contractual tenancy has come to an end, on the following grounds (1954 Act, s 12, Sched 3; 1967 Act, Sched 7):

(*a*) That suitable alternative accommodation will be available for the tenant on the date of the termination of the tenancy. This ground is subject to the restrictions placed on the similar ground available in respect of regulated tenancies.

(*b*) That the tenant has failed to comply with any term of the tenancy as to payment of rent or rates or as to insuring or keeping insured any premises.

(*c*) That the tenant, his sub-tenant, or any person lodging or residing with him has been guilty of nuisance or annoyance to adjoining occupiers, or has been convicted of using any of the premises for illegal or immoral purposes or allowing them to be so used. In the case of a sub-tenant or lodger being guilty, the tenant must also have failed to take reasonable steps to secure his removal.

(*d*) That the premises are reasonably required by the landlord for occupation as his own residence, or that of any son or daughter over the age of eighteen years, or his father or mother or his father-in-law or mother-in-law. This ground is only available if the landlord for the purpose of the Act is the tenant's immediate landlord at the date of termination, if his interest was not purchased or created after 18 February 1966, and if in all the circumstances greater hardship would not be caused by granting possession than by refusing it (1967 Act, Sched 3, para 1).

Where the landlord is a public authority, it may also recover possession on the ground that it proposes to demolish or reconstruct the whole or a substantial part of the premises otherwise than for investment (1967 Act, s 38 (1)). The authorities concerned are those listed on pp 135–6. In proceedings for possession, a certificate of a Minister of the Crown is conclusive that the premises are so required.

2 During the statutory tenancy

During the statutory tenancy the grounds on which the landlord may obtain possession are the same as those normally applicable to regulated tenancies with the following variations.

There are two grounds on which possession cannot be
obtained by reason only of acts or defaults which occurred
before the contractual tenancy terminated (1954 Act, s 10 (2)),
namely:

(a) non-payment of rent and breach of any obligation of
the tenancy; and

(b) nuisance or annoyance caused by the tenant or others
living with him, or use of the premises for immoral or illegal
purposes.

Two additional grounds for possession are available:

(i) failure of the tenant to pay any sums due to the landlord for initial repairs carried out by the landlord but neces-
sitated by the tenant's previous failure to comply with his
obligations (1954 Act, Sched 1, para 17); and

(ii) failure of the tenant to carry out any initial repairs
which are his responsibility by agreement or order of the
court (1954 Act, Sched 2, para 4).

Chapter VIII
Assured Tenancies

Statutes referred to in this chapter:
Landlord and Tenant Act 1954: '1954 Act.'
Housing Act 1980: '1980 Act.'

The rules governing assured tenancies are derived from those relating to business tenancies, contained in Pt II of the 1954 Act. They are only set out here in outline, and the procedure for applying to the court for a new tenancy is not dealt with. In its application to business tenancies, the legislation is considered in Aldridge, *Letting Business Premises* (Oyez Publishing Ltd).

A — EXTENT OF CONTROL

This control applies if the answer to the following four questions is Yes.

(1) *Since the tenancy was granted, has the landlord been an approved body?* (1980 Act, s 56 (3) *(a)*, (4))

An approved body is one which is listed in an order of the Secretary of State, or which falls within a class specified in such an order.

The effect of the landlord ceasing to be an approved body varies, depending on how this comes about. If the reason is a variation in the list of bodies for the time being approved, then the answer to this question remains Yes, both in relation to the current tenancy and to any subsequent one granted by the landlord to the then sitting tenant (1980 Act, s 57 (1)). If the landlord ceases to be an approved body for any other reason, the tenancy becomes, as the case may be, a regulated tenancy or a housing association tenancy (1980 Act, s 57 (2)). The only exception is if, within three months, the landlord's interest is again vested in an approved body.

(2) *Did construction work start on the premises, and any build-*

ing of which they form part, after 8 August 1980? (1980 Act,
s 56 (3) *(b)*)

(3) *Whenever any part of the premises was occupied as a resi-
    dence before the current tenancy, was it occupied under any
    assured tenancy?* (1980 Act, s 56 (3) *(c)*)

(4) *But for the fact that the letting is an assured tenancy, would
    it otherwise have qualified either as a regulated tenancy or
    as a housing association tenancy?* (1980 Act, s 56 (1) *(a)*)

An approved body can grant a protected tenancy or a housing
association tenancy, instead of an assured tenancy, if it wishes.
To do so, it must serve notice on the tenant before the tenancy
is granted (1980 Act, s 56 (6),(7)). That notice must comply with
requirements laid down by regulations.

B — RENT TO BE CHARGED

There is no restriction on the amount of rent that can be
charged under an assured tenancy.

When the tenant renews an assured tenancy, under his statutory rights, the rent under the new tenancy is 'the rent . . . at
which, having regard to the terms of the tenancy (other than
those relating to rent), the [property comprised in the tenancy]
might reasonably be expected to be let in the open market by a
willing lessor' (1954 Act, s 34; 1980 Act, Sched 5, paras 3, 6).
This must be calculated disregarding two matters. First, the
occupation of the premises by the tenant or his predecessors in
title is disregarded. Secondly, one must ignore any improvement
carried out by the tenant for the time being during the twenty-
one years before the renewal application. This applies in cases
where the premises have ever since been comprised in assured
tenancies, and at the termination of each such tenancy the tenant
did not quit.

C — SECURITY OF TENURE

An assured tenancy, whether granted for a fixed term or as a
periodic tenancy, does not come to an end unless one party
gives notice to the other (1954 Act, s 24). To this, there are two
exceptions. First, the tenant may surrender, as long as he has

been in occupation as tenant for at least a month when the instrument was executed or the agreement to surrender was made. Secondly, the landlord may forfeit the tenancy if he is given powers to do so.

The tenant has security of tenure as a result of this extension of the tenancy, coupled with the right to claim a new tenancy in all but seven specified cases.

The landlord and the tenant can jointly apply to the court for an order excluding the statutory renewal provisions (1954 Act, s 38 (4)).

1 Notice by landlord

The landlord can bring an assured tenancy to an end on or after the term date of a fixed term tenancy (1954 Act, s 25). In the case of a periodic tenancy, the notice must take effect on or after the first date on which it could have been terminated by notice to quit. He must give at least six months' and not more than twelve months' notice in the prescribed form.

2 Notice by tenant

There are three ways in which a tenant can bring an assured tenancy to an end by notice. The first applies if he wishes to exercise his right to renew. He can serve a prescribed form of tenant's request for a new tenancy (1954 Act, s 26). This must give at least six months' but not more than twelve months' notice. The date it takes effect must be on or after either the term date of a fixed term tenancy or the first date on which a periodic tenancy could then be ended by notice to quit. This only applies where the assured tenancy was granted for a term certain exceeding one year, or a term of years and thereafter from year to year.

The notice served by a tenant who does not wish to renew his assured tenancy varies depending on the nature of that tenancy. If it was granted for a fixed term, he must give at least three months' notice, to end on the term date or any quarter day thereafter (1954 Act, s 27). A periodic tenancy may be ended by notice to quit, provided that the tenant has been in occupation as tenant for at least a month when he serves it (1954 Act, s 24 (2)).

D — GROUNDS FOR POSSESSION

1 Opposition to renewal

If the tenant claims a new tenancy, there are seven grounds upon which the landlord can oppose his application (1954 Act, ss 30, 31A; 1980 Act, Sched 5, paras 4, 5)

(a) *Dilapidations.* The state of repair of the premises resulting from the tenant's failure to comply with his obligations under the current tenancy.

(b) *Rent arrears.* The tenant has persistently delayed in paying rent when due.

(c) *Other breaches.* Other substantial breaches of the tenant's obligations under the current tenancy, or other reasons connected with his use or management of the premises.

(d) *Alternative accommodation.* The landlord has offered to provide or secure suitable alternative accommodation. The suitability is judged in two ways. First, as regards security of tenure, it must be let on an assured, protected or secure tenancy, or on terms the court considers to be reasonably equivalent. Secondly, it must be reasonably suitable as regards the tenant's means, and his needs and those of his family as to: extent (statutory overcrowding automatically rules out premises), character, furniture (if previously provided) and proximity to place of work.

(e) *Uneconomic sub-letting.* This applies where the current letting was a sub-letting of part only of premises comprised in a head lease. A head landlord, from whom a new tenancy is claimed, can resist the application if he would receive substantially more rent by letting as a whole all the premises comprised in the head lease.

(f) *Demolition and reconstruction.* The landlord intends to demolish or reconstruct the premises, or a substantial part of them, or to carry out substantial construction work on them. The tenant can prevent the landlord from succeeding on this ground by offering him facilities for doing the work, as long as there is not substantial interference with the use of the premises as a residence by the tenant and his family.

(g) *Own occupation.* The landlord intends to occupy the premises as his residence, or for his business. This ground for possession cannot be used by a landlord who purchased the premises within the previous five years.

2 Compensation

A tenant who is refused a new tenancy on one or more of the grounds *(e)*, *(f)*, or *(g)*, set out in the last section, is entitled to compensation from the landlord equal to the rateable value of the premises (1954 Act, s 37; 1980 Act, Sched 5, paras 7, 8). Any contract purporting to exclude this right is void.

Chapter IX
Farmworkers' Houses

Statutes referred to in this chapter:
Rent (Agriculture) Act 1976: '1976 Act.'
Housing Act 1980: '1980 Act.'

A — EXTENT OF CONTROL

The protection of this control extends both to tenants and to licensees, and the Act names them 'protected occupiers'. Statutory tenancies arise on the termination of both types of protected occupancy. For convenience, the terms 'tenant' and 'tenancy' are used below, but they must be read, where the context permits, as also meaning 'licensee' and 'licence'.

In some cases where the control does not apply, there may nevertheless be some protection for tenants against eviction: see pp 113–15.

The control applies if the answer to the following four questions is Yes.

(1) *Is the tenant employed in agriculture, or was he so employed at any time during the tenancy?* (1976 Act, ss 1, 2; Sched 3)

The tenant must be, or have been, a 'qualifying worker'; this means having been employed (or 'working as a permit worker', with a permit under the Agricultural Wages Act 1948, s 5) in agriculture and incidental activities anywhere in the European Economic Community for at least 35 hours a week for not less than 91 out of the last 104 weeks. That employment can be by more than one employer. Weeks of absence by consent, on holiday or sick leave, and weeks where the working hours are less than 35 by arrangement with the employer, still count as full-time employment.

'Agriculture' is defined to include:

(*a*) dairy-farming, and livestock keeping and breeding

(livestock includes birds – other than game birds: *Norman-ton* v *Giles* [1980] 1 WLR 28 – but not fish, and means animals kept for the production of food, wool, skins or fur);

(*b*) production of consumable produce for sale, consumption or other use for trade or business or any other undertaking, even if not for profit: this can include research establishments growing crops for experiment and educational institutions growing food for their own kitchens;

(*c*) grazing, meadow and pasture land, orchard and osier land;

(*d*) market gardens and nurseries;

(*e*) forestry: this is in turn defined to include tree nurseries and woodlands ancillary to other agricultural purposes. Work in forestry before 1 October 1977 (or the commencement date of s 73 of the 1980 Act, in the case of tenants of the Duchies of Lancaster or Cornwall or the Crown Estate Commissioners) is ignored.

Protection is extended to former workers. They still qualify if, when working full-time, they were incapacitated from such full-time work by an injury arising out of or in the course of agricultural employment, or any injury or disease prescribed under the Social Security Act 1975, s 76 (2) (1976 Act, Sched 3, para 2).

(2) *Is the landlord now, or at any time during the tenancy was the then landlord, the tenant's employer in his agricultural employment, or has the employer made arrangements with the landlord to house his agricultural employees?* (1976 Act, s 2 (1), Sched 3, para 3)

(3) *Is the tenancy one which, although not a protected tenancy, would have been one, if that protection had extended:*
    (*a*) *to tenancies at a low rent and*
    (*b*) *to dwelling-houses on agricultural holdings occupied by a person responsible for the farming?* (1976 Act, Sched 2)

This is what the Act calls a 'relevant tenancy'. A licence is within the control if, making the assumption that it is a tenancy and not a licence, the answer to this question is Yes. That is then a 'relevant licence'. A tenancy cannot be a relevant tenancy if it falls within the control on long tenancies (Chapter

VII), or the control relating to business tenancies (Landlord and Tenant Act 1954, Pt II), or if it is a tenancy of an agricultural holding.

Although a bona fide term of the tenancy requiring the landlord to provide the tenant with board excludes this control, that does not include meals provided to the tenant in the course of his employment (1976 Act, Sched 2, para 3 (3), (4)).

(4) *Does the tenant have exclusive occupation of the premises?* (1976 Act, Sched 2)

This bare requirement is modified by provisions substantially identical, although with one exception, to s 22 of the Rent Act 1977, relating to sharing with persons other than the landlord (pp 59–60) (1976 Act, s 23). The exception is intended to cover hostel type accommodation. The control does not apply where there is sharing, and the premises consist of only one room in a building containing at least three other rooms let, or available for letting, as residential accommodation for separate occupiers.

Even if the answer to questions (1) and (2) above is No, the tenancy may still fall within this control if the answer to one of the following three questions is Yes.

(5) *Immediately before the current tenancy was granted, did the tenant occupy the premises under a tenancy for which the answer to questions (1) and (2) would have been Yes?* (1976 Act, s 2 (3) (a))

(6) *Was the current tenancy granted in consideration of the tenant giving up possession of other premises, in respect of which the answers to questions (1)–(4) would have been Yes?* (1976 Act, s 2 (3) (b))

(7) *Did the protected tenancy (for which questions (1)–(4) could have been answered Yes) pass to the present tenant by succession on the death of the original tenant?* (1976 Act, s 3 (2), (3))

The protected occupancy passes, primarily, to the original tenant's spouse living there at the date of the death (1980 Act, s 76 (3)). If there was none, a member of the tenant's family living there for six months immediately prior to the death can succeed. Presumably this provision will be interpreted in the same way as the similar provision of the Rent Act 1977 (p 18). Protection extends to the successor even if he is granted a new tenancy or licence of the same premises, or one of other premises in consideration of giving up possession of the original premises (1976 Act, s 3 (4)).

There is only one statutory transmission, unlike regulated tenancies where two are possible.

B — RENT TO BE CHARGED

No special provisions for fixing or limiting rent apply until a statutory tenancy arises. The rent (if any) then payable is:

(a) Nil, until an agreement or a notice of increase takes effect (1976 Act, s 10 (2));

(b) The sum (if any) provided in an agreement between landlord and tenant (1976 Act, s 11);

(c) On the landlord serving a notice of increase, either before there is an agreement or bringing an agreement to an end, the registered rent if there is one (1976 Act, s 14), otherwise a rent based on rateable value (1976 Act, s 12).

1 Agreement

There is a limit on the amount of rent payable under an agreement. It may not exceed (1976 Act, s 11 (3), (4)):

(a) the registered rent for the premises;

(b) if none is registered: the equivalent of an annual rate of 1½ times the rateable value of the premises at the date the agreement, or the first of a series of agreements, took effect (1976 Act, s 12 (9)).

To those limits, rates may be added, if they are paid by the landlord or the superior lessor (1976 Act, Sched 5, para 11).

An agreement may be made at any time, even before the statutory tenancy begins. Unless it states otherwise, it is terminable by either party on giving at least four weeks' notice. A notice of increase can terminate it. It can also be varied by a further agreement (1976 Act, s 11 (2), (6)–(8)).

Even though an agreement has been terminated, it continues

to have effect if no rent is then payable under a notice of increase (1976 Act, s 11 (9), (11)).

2 Rent based on rateable value

In the absence of a registered rent, the rent payable on a landlord's notice of increase taking effect is at the annual rate equal to 1½ times the rateable value when the notice is served (1976 Act, s 12). If the premises have no separate rateable value, there must be an apportionment or aggregation, either estimated by the landlord or conclusively determined by the county court. To calculate a weekly or monthly rent, a month is treated as one-twelfth of a year and a week as one fifty-second part (1976 Act, s 17).

3 Registered rent

Application to register the rent of a statutory tenancy which follows a protected occupancy can be made to the rent officer, as in the case of a regulated tenancy (1976 Act, s 13). A special form of application is prescribed (Rent (Agriculture) (Rent Registration) Regulations 1978). The rent is registered in a separate part of the register. Registration of a rent in any other part of the register is equally effective to limit the rent payable under this type of statutory tenancy, but it does not prevent an application to register a new rent within two years of that other registration.

Certain parts of the general registration procedure do not apply to these cases, namely certificates of fair rent, applications to cancel registration and applications by the local authority.

Phasing applies to rent increases on a second and subsequent registration (1976 Act, s 15). The rules follow the two-year phasing provisions for regulated tenancies (1976 Act, Sched 6; 1980 Act, s 60 (3)).

4 Notice of increase

A notice of increase, whether for payment of a rent based on rateable value or a registered rent, may be served before the statutory tenancy begins. It terminates the protected occupancy, if a notice to quit served at the same time could have terminated it before the notice of increase took effect (1976 Act, s 16 (2), (3)).

A notice of increase must specify the amount of rent to be paid and the date it takes effect. That date may not be earlier than four weeks before it is served (1976 Act, ss 12 (3), (4), 14 (3)). The notice can take effect from the termination of an agreement as to the rent payable. If it does, it must say so, and specify the rent last payable under the agreement. If a notice is served while an agreement is still in force it can operate to terminate the agreement, when two conditions are satisfied. The date on which it states it takes effect must be both after the date of service of the notice, and a date on which the landlord could have terminated the agreement by notice served then.

The county court has power to amend any notice of increase in two cases. First, if it is satisfied that the landlord made a bona fide error which would invalidate it. Secondly, if the rent was calculated on the landlord's estimate of rateable value, in which case the court can amend the amount of the rent (1976 Act, s 16 (4)–(7)). Such an amendment may be made on terms. If an amendment results in an increase in rent, it is not recoverable in respect of any period more than six months before the date of the amending order.

5 Terms for payment

The implied terms of a statutory tenancy include a covenant to pay rent (1976 Act, s 10 (3)–(5)). Subject to an agreement between landlord and tenant, rent is payable weekly in arrears, unless rent or an equivalent payment was made in advance under the protected occupancy. The day for rent payments, if they are to be made in arrear, is:

(a) the day payments were made under the protected occupancy; or if none

(b) if the tenant receives a weekly wage when the protected occupancy ends, his pay day; or if none

(c) Friday, or such other day as landlord and tenant agree.

6 Rates

Except where an agreement relating to rent is in force, the landlord may recover from a statutory tenant as rent, any rates borne by him or a superior lessor (1976 Act, Sched 5, para 11). The landlord must serve notice on the tenant, and it cannot take effect more than four weeks before service. If the premises are rated as part of a larger hereditament, the tenant's proportion must be agreed in writing or determined by the county court.

7 Excess rent

The same provisions for the recovery of overpaid rent, and entries in rent books showing irrecoverable sums as arrears, apply here as for regulated tenancies (1976 Act, s 21 (1)–(4)).

C — SECURITY OF TENURE

When a protected occupancy comes to an end, a statutory tenancy immediately arises, and continues so long as the tenant occupies the premises as his residence (1976 Act, s 4). The nature of the statutory tenant's occupation must be such as would qualify him for a statutory regulated tenancy. A statutory tenancy can pass once by transmission on the death of the tenant.

A statutory tenancy under the 1976 Act is different from the normal continuation of a protected tenancy, because the protected occupancy which it extends may not itself have been a tenancy. The former contractual terms may not, therefore, cover all the matters that a tenancy agreement should. The 1976 Act consequently makes express provision as to the terms of the statutory tenancy.

1 Terms of statutory tenancy

The original contract terms, including any implied, continue to apply under the statutory tenancy, except any that make the tenant's right to occupy depend on his employment in agriculture (1976 Act, Sched 5). The statutory terms do not reduce the tenant's rights under the contractual ones. By agreement, landlord and tenant can vary the statutory terms, although not for any of the following purposes: substantially to increase the premises let; to prejudice any obligation implied by law (eg, repairing); to change the circumstances in which the tenant can give notice to quit; or to include any term relating to employment, or unrelated to occupation of the dwelling-house.

If the contractual terms granted a licence, the statutory tenancy is to be a weekly tenancy, and the tenant must give a minimum of four weeks' notice to quit.

The landlord's obligations are: the provision of services or facilities (other than access) which he can reasonably provide, and did previously provide although not necessarily immediately before the start of the statutory tenancy, and which the tenant cannot reasonably be expected to provide for himself; repairs in accordance with the Housing Act 1961, s 32; and a covenant for quiet enjoyment. The tenant's obligations are to use the premises in a tenant-like manner and only as a private dwelling-house; an absolute bar on assignment, sub-letting and parting with possession; and to allow the landlord access for the repairs which are his responsibility.

The landlord can in two cases remove or restrict the access to the premises, provided there is an alternative (1976 Act, Sched 5, para 9 (5), (6)). This can be done temporarily to prevent the spread of disease in crops or livestock, and either temporarily or permanently in the interests of efficient agriculture.

2 Sub-tenants

A protected occupier or statutory tenant who is a lawful sub-tenant enjoys protection in the same circumstances as a protected regulated tenant in that position (1976 Act, s 9).

3 Matrimonial home

A statutory tenancy of a matrimonial home can be transferred to one spouse from the other or both jointly by order of a divorce court, in the same way as a statutory regulated tenancy (Matrimonial Homes Act 1967, s 7 (3A); 1976 Act, Sched 8, para 16).

D — GROUNDS FOR POSSESSION

The grounds on which a court may order possession against a protected occupier or a statutory tenant are divided into two: discretionary and mandatory. In discretionary cases, the court may only make the order if it considers it reasonable to do so, and has further powers (1976 Act, s 7). It may, for as long as it sees fit, stay or suspend execution or postpone the date of pos-

session. An order may be granted on terms, and if conditions
are satisfied, the court may discharge or rescind the order for
possession.

The grounds for possession under the 1976 Act closely follow
those relating to regulated tenancies. They are listed below
merely by headings with notes as to variations.

1 Discretionary grounds

(a) Suitable alternative accommodation, not provided or
arranged by the local authority (Case I).

(b) Suitable alternative accommodation provided or
arranged by the local authority (Case II). The offer by the
local authority is not conclusive, as it is in the case of regulated tenancies. The court must be satisfied that the alternative accommodation was reasonably suited to the needs of
the tenant and his family as regards proximity to place of
work and extent, and reasonably suitable to the tenant's
means. The offer must be open for at least fourteen days,
but not necessarily until the court hearing. The tenant must
show that he acted reasonably in not accepting it.

(c) Failure to pay rent, or breach of obligation (Case III).

(d) Nuisance, annoyance or illegal or immoral use (Case
IV).

(e) Deterioration in the condition of the premises (Case
V).

(f) Deterioration in the condition of furniture (Case VI).

(g) Tenant's notice to quit (Case VII). This does not
apply where all that the tenant did was to give notice to
terminate his employment, and that operated to terminate
his tenancy.

(h) The tenant assigned, sub-let or parted with possession
of all or part of the premises after the operative date without
the landlord's consent (Case VIII). This is not restricted, as
it is in the case of regulated tenancies, to cases resulting in
the whole premises being sub-let. The operative date is:

Lettings by the Duchy of Lancaster, the Duchy of
Cornwall or the Crown Estate Commissioners subsisting when s 73 of the 1980 Act came into force: that
commencement date:

other lettings to workers in forestry: 1 October 1977; other lettings: 1 January 1977.

(*i*) Premises required for landlord or family (Case IX). Family is extended to include a grandparent of the landlord or his spouse. The landlord must not have purchased the premises, or any interest in them, after 12 April 1976.

(*j*) Overcharging sub-tenants (Case X). Charging more than the recoverable rent under the 1976 Act is included. The overcharging must relate to a rental period beginning on or after the operative date (as for Case VIII).

2 Mandatory grounds

(*a*) Owner-occupier requiring possession (Case XI). In the case of a tenancy subsisting on 1 January 1977, notice must have been given before 1 July 1977 (in the case of premises let to a worker in forestry, the dates are respectively 1 October 1977 and 1 April 1978). Otherwise, notices must be given before the tenancy starts.

(*b*) Retirement home (Case XII). Notice to the tenant must be given as for the preceding case.

(*c*) Overcrowding (Case XIII).

Chapter X
Servicemen's Accommodation

Statutes referred to in this chapter:
Reserve and Auxiliary Forces (Protection of Civil Interests)
Act 1951: '1951 Act.'
Rent (Agriculture) Act 1976: '1976 Act.'
Rent Act 1977: '1977 Act.'
Housing Act 1980: '1980 Act.'

A — EXTENT OF CONTROL

If the answer to all the following questions is Yes, some measure of control and protection is granted by the 1951 Act.

The 1951 Act was slightly amended by the 1977 Act, Sched 23, so that its wording takes into account the consolidation effected by the 1977 Act.

(1) *Is the 'tenant' a volunteer or conscripted serviceman (which includes servicewoman) serving otherwise than on a regular engagement?*

Protection is extended to a serviceman living with dependants in premises rent free or under licence granted by his employer in consequence of his employment (1951 Act, s 18; 1976 Act, Sched 8, para 1). 'Tenant' is hereafter used in that extended sense. This does not apply where the tenant occupies on-licensed premises (1951 Act, s 18 (3)).

(2) *Except in case of short training only (see below) does one of the following reasons prevent the tenancy being protected?* (1951 Act, s 16)

(*a*) That the rateable value of the premises exceeds the limits of the Rent Act jurisdiction.

(*b*) That the reversion immediately expectant on the serviceman's tenancy belongs to a local authority, a development corporation, the Commission for the New Towns, the

Development Board for Rural Wales, a housing trust or the Housing Corporation.

(c) That the premises were let with more than two acres of agricultural land, but are not an 'agricultural holding'.

(d) That the rent is less than two-thirds of the appropriate rateable value.

(3) *Were the premises occupied as a residence by the serviceman and at least one dependant immediately before his service started, and are they still occupied by the dependant(s) with or without him?*

Dependants include the wife or husband, and any other member of the family wholly or mainly maintained by the serviceman immediately before his service started (1951 Act, ss 23 (1), 64 (2)).

This control does not apply where the premises are bona fide let at a rent which includes payments for board, are subject to a protected occupancy or a statutory tenancy under the 1976 Act, or are on-licensed premises (1951 Act, s 14 (2); 1976 Act, Sched 8, para 1).

One further question must be asked: *for how long is the service due to last?*

If it is voluntary or obligatory service, for training only, for at least seven consecutive days, but limited to less than three months, it is classed as 'short service' (1951 Act, s 64 (1), Sched 1, paras 2, 6, 7). Only limited protection is given in such cases. Other cases are dealt with under the heading 'Long Service'.

In cases of long service, where the serviceman's family residence is subject to a pre-1980 Act restricted contract, any notice to quit is treated as extended as if it had been referred to a rent tribunal, even though there has been no such reference (1951 Act, s 15; 1980 Act, Sched 25, para 1).

Where accommodation is shared with someone other than the landlord, the control applicable to such cases applies in cases of long service to make the tenancy protected until four months after the end of the service, where for one of the reasons given under question (2) above it would not otherwise have applied (1951 Act, s 17).

B — Long Service

1 Rent to be charged

The rent during any period of statutory protection is the rent payable for the last rental period of the tenancy, subject to any adjustments that could be applied for rates, services and furniture to the rent under a regulated statutory tenancy before registration of the rent. The rent cannot, however, be increased beyond any limit imposed by an agreement between the parties (1951 Act, s 16 (4), (5); 1980 Act, Sched 25, para 2).

2 Security of tenure

For a period until four months after the service finishes the security afforded to controlled tenancies applies to the serviceman's dwelling. Two additional restrictions on obtaining possession apply (1951 Act, s 20):

(a) Where one of the serviceman's obligations under his tenancy was carrying out duties in connection with his employment, and he is prevented from doing so by his service, that failure is not treated as a breach justifying an order for possession.

(b) Subject to a limitation in two cases, the power to order possession without alternative accommodation being available where the landlord requires the premises for a new employee does not apply. The limitation is that the court may, in considering making an order for possession without alternative accommodation, take into account the circumstances in the following cases:

(i) that the landlords are statutory undertakers, a local authority or a development corporation having public utility functions, and require the premises for a full-time employee in connection with those functions (definitions: 1951 Act, s 20 (4));

(ii) that the tenant immediately before his period of service was a policeman and the premises are required for the occupation of another policeman.

C — Short Service

1 Rent to be charged

There is no control of rent in the case of short service.

2 Security of tenure

During the period of service and for fourteen days thereafter, no order for possession can be enforced, nor any right of re-entry exercised, without leave of the court (1951 Act, s 25 (1)). On an application, the court may refuse leave, or grant it subject to such restrictions and conditions as it thinks proper, if it thinks that by reason of circumstances directly or indirectly attributable to the tenant's service immediate enforcement would not be right (1951 Act, s 25 (2)).

Chapter XI
Housing Association Tenancies

Statutes referred to in this chapter:
Rent Act 1977: '1977 Act.'
Housing Act 1980: '1980 Act.'

Lettings by housing associations, housing trusts and the Housing Corporation are subject to two separate controls. The control dealt with in this Chapter imposes a limit on rent, but gives tenants no security of tenure. The lettings also fall within the category of secure tenancies (Chapter XII), which confers security of tenure, but does not control the rent the landlord may charge.

A — Extent of Control

This control applies if the answers to the following five questions are Yes.

(1) *Is the landlord a housing association, a housing trust or the Housing Corporation?* (1977 Act, s 86 (2) *(a)*)

For this purpose a housing association is a society, body of trustees or company established, whether exclusively or not, for constructing or improving houses or for managing, facilitating or encouraging those activities. It may not trade for profit, and its constitution must prohibit paying interest or dividends to holders of loan share capital in excess of a rate prescribed by the Treasury (Housing Act 1957, s 189 (1)). However, there is excluded any association to which the Secretary of State has, by order, applied provisions relating to local authorities, eg, the North Eastern Housing Association (1980 Act, Sched 10, para 1 (3)).

A housing trust is a corporation or body of persons required to devote either all its funds to the provision of housing accommodation, or the whole or substantially the whole of its funds to charitable purposes, in fact using them to provide housing accommodation (1977 Act, ss 15 (5), 86 (4); 1980 Act, s 74 (2), Sched 10, para 1 (5)).

(2) *If the landlord is a housing association, is it registered under the Housing Act 1974, s 13?* (1977 Act, s 15 (3) *(a)*)

(3) *Is the letting outside the category of co-ownership tenancy?* (1977 Act, s 86 (2), (3A); 1980 Act, Sched 10, para 1 (2), (4))

A co-ownership tenancy is one granted by an association registered under the Industrial and Provident Societies Act 1965, with rules restricting membership to tenants and tenancies to members. It entitles the tenant, or his personal representatives, to a sum calculated directly or indirectly by reference to the value of the premises, on ceasing to be a member.

(4) *But for the identity of the landlord, would the tenancy be regulated?* (1977 Act, s 86 (2) *(b)*)

(5) *Is the letting for wholly non-business purposes?* (1977 Act, s 86 (2) *(b)*)

If the Landlord and Tenant Act 1954, Pt II, applies, this control does not.

B — Rent to be Charged

1 Registered rent

The registration procedure applicable to regulated tenancies applies to premises let, available or to become available for letting, under tenancies to which this control applies, except that registrations are recorded in a separate part of the register (1977 Act, s 87). The absence of security of tenure for the tenant is not a ground for assessing a lower fair rent than would otherwise have been appropriate (*Palmer* v *Peabody Trust* [1975] QB 604). When a rent is registered, whether in respect of a letting by landlords within this control or a regulated tenancy, that is the maximum chargeable, plus any amount of general and water rates borne by the landlord or any superior landlord (1977 Act, s 88 (1), (3)). The registration can be subject to variation with the cost to the landlord of services, maintenance and repairs (1977 Act, ss 71 (4), 87 (2)).

Any increase in rent on a fresh registration is subject to phasing over two years in the same way as for regulated tenancies, unless no tenancy is subsisting at the date of registration (1977 Act, s 89; 1980 Act, Sched 10, para 2).

2 Before registration

If no rent is registered, the calculation of the rent limit depends upon to which of the following three questions the answer is Yes (1977 Act, s 88 (4), (6), (7); 1980 Act, Sched 25, para 40).

(1) *Was the tenancy created by a lease or agreement made prior to 1 January 1973?*

The rent limit is the rent reserved by the tenancy, as varied by any agreement made before 1 January 1973.

(2) *In any other case, were the premises let within the two years before the commencement of the tenancy?*

The rent limit is the rent for the last rental period of the previous tenancy, plus any increase since that date in general and water rates borne by the landlord or any superior landlord. A previous tenancy is to be ignored if it commenced during the currency of conditions imposed under the Housing (Financial Provisions) Act 1924, s 2, the Housing (Rural Workers) Act 1926, s 3, the Housing (Financial Provisions) Act 1938, s 3, the Housing Act 1949, s 23, the Housing Act 1952, s 3, the Housing Act 1957, s 104 (3), or the Housing (Financial Provisions) Act 1958, s 46 (1). The landlord must supply information about previous tenancies if the tenant so requests in writing.

(3) *Is the case one falling outside the previous two classes?*

The rent limit is the rent reserved by the lease or agreement creating the tenancy, but not as varied by any subsequent agreement. The normal form of rent review clause, for adjustment of the rent to the current market level, is thus ineffective.

3 Notices of increase

The rent payable under a periodic tenancy within this control can be increased by service of a notice which does not operate as a notice to quit (1977 Act, s 93; 1980 Act, Sched 10, para 5). This applies whenever the tenancy was granted. The notice must be in writing and give the date on which it takes effect. It must be served at least four weeks before that date.

The tenant can render a notice of increase ineffective by giving notice to quit before the notice of increase takes effect. The tenant can withdraw his notice to quit, with the landlord's written agreement, before the date for the rent increase, and that reactivates the original notice of increase.

4 Excess rent

Any rent paid over the rent limits laid down under this control is recoverable in the same ways as excess rent paid under a regulated tenancies, and the same provisions about excessive rent book entries apply (1977 Act, s 94).

Chapter XII
Secure Tenancies

Statute referred to in this chapter:
Housing Act 1980: '1980 Act.'

A — EXTENT OF CONTROL

This control gives security of tenure, but does not impose any limit on the rent that can be charged. Some tenancies may, however, be both secure tenancies and housing association tenancies, the control of which does extend to rent. This control applies to licences as it does to tenancies (1980 Act, s 48) and 'tenancy', 'landlord' and 'tenant' must be read with appropriately extended meanings. The only exception is that a licence granted as a temporary expedient to a squatter, on the same or other premises, is not a secure tenancy.

This control applies if the answer to the following eight questions is Yes.

(1) *Is the landlord one of the specified public authorities or housing bodies?* (1980 Act, ss 28 (2), (4), 49 (1), (2))

The specified authorities and bodies are:

(*a*) a local authority, ie, a district or London borough council, the Greater London Council, the Common Council of the City of London or the Council of the Isles of Scilly (1980 Act, s 50 (1));

(*b*) a county council, where the tenancy was granted in exercise of its reserve powers to provide housing on behalf of a district council;

(*c*) the Commission for the New Towns;

(*d*) a development corporation;

(*e*) the Development Board for Rural Wales;

(*f*) the Housing Corporation;

(*g*) a charitable housing trust (defined: pp 86–7);

(*h*) a housing association which is registered by the Housing Corporation, or is one that restricts membership to tenants and tenancies to members and is registered under the Industrial and Provident Societies Act 1965. A tenancy granted by an association with those restrictions in its rules, and registered under both provisions, is not a secure tenancy;

(i) a housing co-operative, where the premises are comprised in a housing co-operative agreement with a local authority, new town corporation or the Development Board for Rural Wales.

(2) *Is the tenancy periodic, or was it granted for a term of 21 years or less?* (1980 Act, Sched 3, para 1)

A tenancy granted so as to become terminable after a death can, with one exception, be a secure tenancy. A perpetually renewable tenancy is not a secure tenancy, unless it is a sub-lease granted out of a lease short enough to qualify.

A tenancy for life is not a secure tenancy if it is a 'shared ownership tenancy'. This is one granted for a premium calculated by reference to a percentage of the value or cost of the premises, by a housing association registered by the Housing Corporation. It must comply with regulations made under s 140 (4) (b) of the 1980 Act.

(3) *Are the premises a dwelling-house let as a separate dwelling?* (1980 Act, s 28 (1))

The definition of a dwelling-house will presumably follow that adopted for Rent Act purposes. The requirement also precludes cases where living accommodation is shared. A tenancy is a secure tenancy even if it was granted before the commencement of the Act introducing this control (1980 Act, s 47).

(4) *Is the tenant an individual who occupies the premises as his only or principal home?* (1980 Act, s 28 (3))

In the case of a joint tenancy, all the tenants must be individuals, but only one need occupy the premises as his only or principal home.

(5) *Are the premises vested in the original tenant, or an authorised successor, and at least partly in his possession?* (1980 Act, ss 30, 37 (1), (2))

On the death of a secure tenant under a periodic tenancy, there can normally be one statutory transmission. An assignment does not cause a tenancy to cease to be secure if it is to someone to whom a statutory transmission could then have taken place, nor if it is pursuant to an order under the Matrimonial Causes Act 1973, s 24.

(6) *Is the tenant outside these categories: employee, homeless person, student, almsperson?* (1980 Act, Sched 3, paras 2, 3, 5, 11, 13)

Two classes of employee must be considered separately: first, those in social service and educational premises, and secondly, other employees.

If the premises are held by the landlord for statutory social service or educational functions and form part of a building held for those purposes, or are in the curtilage of one, a tenancy on terms that it ends when the tenant's employment by the landlord comes to an end is not a secure tenancy. In this case, occupation of the premises need not be a term of the tenant's employment.

In the case of an employee in any other job, he is not a secure tenant if his contract of employment or apprenticeship requires him to occupy the premises for the better performance of his duties, and he is employed either by the landlord or by:

(a) a local authority, ie, a county, district or London borough council, the Greater London Council, the Common Council of the City of London or the Council of the Isles of Scilly;

(b) a development corporation;

(c) the Commission for the New Towns;

(d) the Development Board for Rural Wales.

Tenancies granted under duties imposed by the Housing (Homeless Persons) Act 1977 are not secure tenancies until twelve months from the council's notification of its decision on the tenant's homelessness or its duty to accommodate him, or earlier if the landlord so notifies the tenant.

Only lettings to allow students to attend courses designated by regulations at a university or establishment of further education fall outside the secure tenancy category, and only when the landlord gives the tenant advance written notice. Six months after the end of the student's course, or his last course, the tenancy becomes secure. If he does not attend the course, it becomes secure six months after it is granted. The landlord can agree to its becoming secure earlier, by notifying the tenant.

A letting to an almsperson is not a secure tenancy if it is a licence granted by an almshouse charity, and the tenant is not obliged to pay more than the maximum contribution to maintenance and essential services from time to time authorised or approved by the Charity Commissioners.

(7) *Were the premises let as permanent accommodation?* (1980 Act, Sched 3, paras 4, 6–8)

Tenants of temporary accommodation are not secure tenants in the following cases:

(*a*) Premises acquired for development let pending that development;

(*b*) Premises let to someone not then resident in that district or London borough to allow him to take work there or to seek permanent accommodation. The tenant must have had a job in the area concerned, or the offer of one, before the tenancy was granted. The landlord has to give the tenant written notice that this exception applies. The tenancy becomes a secure tenancy if it continues for a year, or earlier if the landlord so notifies the tenant;

(*c*) Premises leased to the landlord with vacant possession for use as temporary housing accommodation, on terms allowing the superior lessor to obtain vacant possession at the expiry of a specified term, or at his option. The superior lessor cannot be a body capable of granting a secure tenancy, and the landlord's only interest in the premises must be under that lease, or as a mortgagee;

(*d*) Premises let while works were carried out on a dwelling-house previously occupied by the tenant, not under a secure tenancy.

(8) *Do the premises fall outside the following categories: agricultural holdings, licensed premises, business premises?* (1980 Act, Sched 3, paras 9, 10, 12)

Agricultural holdings are defined on p 7. Licensed premises are those with an on-licence (p 7). Business premises are those of which the tenancy falls within Pt II of the Landlord and Tenant Act 1954.

B — Security of Tenure

1 Termination of secure tenancy

When a fixed term secure tenancy comes to an end, a periodic tenancy of the premises automatically arises by statute, unless the landlord immediately grants the tenant a new secure tenancy (1980 Act, s 29 (1)). This applies whether the secure tenancy ends by effluxion of time, or on the operation of a proviso for re-entry or forfeiture without an order for possession. This is the equivalent of the statutory tenancy that arises on the termination of a protected tenancy.

A periodic secure tenancy – originally granted as a weekly, monthly, etc, tenancy – can only be ended by a court order for possession (1980 Act, s 32 (1)). The same applies to a landlord seeking to exercise an option prematurely to terminate a secure tenancy granted for a fixed term.

2 Statutory periodic tenancy

A periodic tenancy arising by statute on the termination of a fixed term secure tenancy is on the same terms as the secure tenancy, with the exception of any incompatible with a periodic tenancy, and excluding any provision for re-entry or forfeiture (1980 Act, s 29 (2)). The parties to the periodic tenancy are those who were the landlord and the tenant at the end of the secure tenancy. The periods of the periodic tenancy are the same as those for which the rent was last payable under the secure tenancy, ie, when rent under the fixed term tenancy was payable monthly, a monthly tenancy arises.

3 Transfer on divorce

A court hearing a divorce or nullity petition may order the transfer of a secure tenancy from one spouse to the other (Matrimonial Homes Act 1967, s 7 (1), (2); 1980 Act, Sched 25, paras 15, 16). Similarly, if the spouses are joint tenants, it may vest the tenancy in one only of them. This jurisdiction must be exercised between the date of granting the decree nisi and when it is made absolute. The former tenant's rights end on the date of the decree absolute.

4 Statutory transmission on death

When the tenant under a periodic secure tenancy dies, including a tenant under a statutory periodic tenancy, the tenancy can be transmitted once only to a member of his family (1980 Act, ss 30 (1), 31). There can be no transmission where the tenant who dies falls into one of the following categories ('successors'):

(a) A tenant who himself received the tenancy by transmission;

(b) A former joint tenant who became sole tenant, including a person who was joint tenant of the fixed term tenancy that preceded a statutory periodic tenancy;

(c) A person who became tenant on assignment (except pursuant to an order under the Matrimonial Causes Act 1973, s 24) or on vesting on the death of a previous tenant.

If a periodic tenancy vested in a successor comes to an end, and within six months he is granted another periodic secure tenancy, he counts as a successor in relation to that second tenancy in either of two cases. The second tenancy cannot be transmitted on his death if it related to the same premises as the previous tenancy, or if it was granted by the same landlord. The tenancy agreement for the second secure tenancy can expressly preclude this effect, and so allow it to be transmitted when the tenant dies.

A member of the tenant's family must occupy the premises as his only or principal home when the tenant dies in order to qualify to succeed him and take the tenancy by transmission (1980 Act, s 30 (2), (3)). The tenant's spouse has preference in succeeding him, and needs no other qualification. Other members of the family must have resided with the tenant, although not necessarily in the premises in question, for the twelve months immediately preceding the tenant's death. If more than one member of the family qualifies, they may decide between them who succeeds. In the absence of agreement, the landlord selects one.

A 'member of the family' means a parent, grandparent, child, grandchild, brother, sister, uncle, aunt, nephew and niece, and someone with whom the tenant lived as man and wife (1980 Act, s 50 (3)). In-laws, stepchildren, illegitimate children and relations of the half-blood are counted as full relations.

5 Preliminary notice of possession proceedings

A landlord who wishes to take possession proceedings against a secure tenant must give a preliminary notice on a prescribed form (1980 Act, s 33). The notice must state the ground on which the court will be asked to order possession, and give particulars. In the case of a periodic secure tenancy, the notice must give a date after which proceedings may be begun, and that cannot be earlier than the date on which the landlord could have ended it by notice to quit but for the statutory provisions. Action must be started within twelve months of that date.

C — GROUNDS FOR POSSESSION

All the grounds for possession of premises let on secure tenancies are discretionary. One or both of two overriding requirements – reasonableness or the availability of suitable alternative accommodation – must be satisfied.

1 Reasonableness

Where reasonableness must be proved, the landlord has to establish that it is reasonable at the date of the hearing for the court to make the order (1980 Act, s 34 (3) *(a)*). Among matters that may be considered are: the conduct of the parties (*Peach* v *Lowe* [1947] 1 All ER 441); hardship to one party (*Williamson* v *Pallant* [1924] 2 KB 173); and the interests of the public (*Cresswell* v *Hodgson* [1951] 2 KB 92).

2 Suitable alternative accommodation

Where a ground for possession is subject to the provision of suitable alternative accommodation, the landlord must show that the accommodation will be available when the order takes effect (1980 Act, s 34 (3) *(b)*). A certificate of a local authority responsible for housing in that area, that it will provide suitable accommodation for the tenant by a specified date, is conclusive except where the landlord is a local authority (1980 Act, Sched 4, Pt II, para 3).

In other cases, the alternative accommodation must satisfy

two criteria (1980 Act, Sched 4, Pt II, paras 1, 2). First, it must consist of a separate dwelling to be let providing suitable security of tenure. This means it must be let on a secure tenancy, or on a protected tenancy under which the landlord cannot recover possession on one of the mandatory grounds.

Secondly, the alternative accommodation must be reasonably suitable for the needs of the tenant and his family. These matters must be taken into account:

(a) the nature of the accommodation that the landlord generally allocates to people with those needs;

(b) the distance from places of work or education;

(c) the distance from the home of any member of the tenant's family, if proximity is essential to his or the tenant's well-being;

(d) the accommodation they need (but disregarding the statutory requirements as to extent if possession is sought on the ground of overcrowding) and their means;

(e) the terms of the current and proposed tenancies;

(f) the furniture to be provided, if furniture was previously included.

3 Grounds subject to reasonableness

The grounds for possession subject to the prior requirement of reasonableness are (1980 Act, s 34 (2) (a), Sched 4, Pt I):

(a) *Ground 1: Breach of obligation.* Non-payment of rent lawfully due, or a breach of an obligation of the tenancy.

(b) *Ground 2: Nuisance, annoyance, etc.* Any of the following acts on the part of the tenant or any person residing in the premises:

    (i) conduct which is a nuisance or annoyance to neighbours;

    (ii) conviction for using or allowing the premises to be used for immoral or illegal purposes.

(c) *Grounds 3 and 4: Dilapidations.* Deterioration in the condition of the premises, the common parts (ie, other parts of the building that the tenant is entitled to use in common with the occupiers of other premises let by the landlord) or of furniture provided by the landlord for use under the tenancy or in the common parts. This must have been caused by the tenant or someone residing in the premises, by waste, neglect or default in relation to the premises, or by ill treatment of the furniture. If a lodger or sub-tenant was responsible, the landlord must also show that the tenant has not taken reasonable steps for his removal.

(d) Ground 5: False statement. The landlord was induced to grant the tenancy to the tenant, alone or jointly with others, by a false statement that the tenant made knowingly or recklessly.

(e) Ground 6: Temporary accommodation. The tenancy was granted to the tenant, or his predecessor, while works were completed on other premises. Those other premises must have been occupied by him as his only or principal home. The works must be finished. The second tenancy must have been granted on the understanding that the tenant would move back when the premises were again available, which they now are.

4 Grounds subject to suitable alternative accommodation

The grounds for possession subject to the landlord showing that suitable alternative accommodation will be available are (1980 Act, s 34 (2) *(b)*, Sched 4, Pt I):

(a) Ground 7: Overcrowding. The premises are overcrowded in such circumstances as to render the occupier guilty of an offence.

(b) Ground 8: Demolition or reconstruction. Within a reasonable time after obtaining possession, the landlord intends to demolish or reconstruct the premises or part of the building in which they are, or carry out other work, which he cannot reasonably do without obtaining possession.

(c) Ground 9: Conflict with charitable objects. Where the landlord is a charity, the tenant's continued occupation of the premises would conflict with the objects of the charity.

5 Grounds subject to reasonableness and suitable alternative accommodation

The grounds for possession where the landlord must establish both reasonableness and the provision of suitable alternative accommodation are (1980 Act, s 34 (2) *(c)*, Sched 4, Pt I):

(a) Ground 10: Accommodation for disabled. Premises for the accommodation of the physically disabled, substantially different from ordinary dwelling-houses, are no longer occupied by any such person and are required for that purpose.

(b) Ground 11: Accommodation for those difficult to house. Premises let by a housing association or housing trust only for occupation by those whose circumstances (other than purely financial circumstances) make it especially difficult to satisfy their housing needs are required for that purpose. They must either be no longer occupied by such a person, or the tenant must have an offer of a secure tenancy from a local authority.

(c) Ground 12: Accommodation for those with special needs. Premises let as one of a group of dwelling-houses for occupation by people with special needs, for whom a social service or special facility is provided nearby, which are no longer occupied by such a person and are required for that purpose.

(d) Ground 13: Surplus accommodation. A member of a deceased tenant's family (but not his spouse) succeeded to the tenancy on a statutory transmission and the accommodation is more extensive than he reasonably requires. The preliminary notice of the possession proceedings must be given at least six months but not more than twelve months after the death of the former tenant.

Chapter XIII
Houses Sold by Local Authorities

Statutes referred to in this chapter:
Housing Act 1957: '1957 Act.'
Rent (Agriculture) Act 1967: '1967 Act.'
Rent Act 1977: '1977 Act.'
Housing Act 1980: '1980 Act.'

A — EXTENT OF CONTROL

When a local authority sells a house it may impose conditions regulating *(inter alia)* the amount of rent charged on a letting. The restriction applies for up to five years, or such longer period as is authorised or required by the Secretary of State (1957 Act, s 104; Housing (Amendment) Act 1973, s 2). The conditions are registrable as local land charges, so that the information is available to all (1957 Act, s 104 (5)). The conditions confer no security of tenure on the tenant.

B — RENT TO BE CHARGED

1 Rent limits

The rent limit varies according to the category into which the letting falls (1977 Act, s 145; 1980 Act, Sched 25, para 52):

(a) Regulated tenancy or housing association tenancy. The rules applicable to regulated tenancies converted from controlled tenancies apply, so that a rent agreement is not valid unless a rent is registered. The former ban on the registration of rents for these tenancies is withdrawn (1980 Act, Sched 26).

(b) Protected occupancy or statutory tenancy under the 1976 Act. The limits applicable under the 1976 Act apply.

(c) Other cases. The maximum rent is as agreed between the landlord and the local authority, or in default of agreement as determined by the Secretary of State.

2 Excess rent

Charging too much rent is an offence punishable on summary conviction by the imposition of a fine of an amount to secure that the offender derives no benefit from the offence, plus £100, or three months' imprisonment, or both (1957 Act, s 104 (4), applying Building Materials and Housing Act 1945, s 7, as amended by Housing Act 1949, s 43).

Chapter XIV
Caravans

Statutes referred to in this chapter:
Caravan Sites Act 1968: '1968 Act.'
Mobile Homes Act 1975: '1975 Act.'

A — EXTENT OF CONTROL

Full Rent Act protection has been withheld from the occupiers of caravans, even when used as residences, but the 1968 and 1975 Acts have given them limited and separate rights, mainly as to security of tenure. The 1975 Act is concerned with those who own and occupy their caravans, and the agreements that they have with the owners of the sites where the caravans are stationed. The 1968 Act is wider, extending to agreements to occupy caravans owned by the site owner, or a third party.

There have also been cases in which lettings of caravans have been held to be restricted contracts, under the jurisdiction of the rent tribunal.

For the control to apply, the answer to the following three questions must be Yes:

(1) *Are the premises a caravan?* (Caravan Sites and Control of Development Act 1960, s 29 (1); 1968 Act, s 13)

A caravan is a structure capable of being moved by towing or being transported on a motor vehicle, or trailer. It must be designed or adapted for human habitation. Two-unit caravans, which cannot legally be transported by road when assembled, are included if no dimension exceeds the following limits: 60 ft long, 20 ft wide and 10 ft high internally. Tents and railway carriages when on the railway are specifically excluded from the definition. The 1975 Act uses the term 'mobile home' but this simply means a caravan as defined above (1975 Act, s 9 (1)).

(2) *Is the caravan stationed on a caravan site licensed for all the year round occupation, not merely holiday use?* (1968

102

Act s 1 (2); 1975 Act, s 9 (1))

The 1968 Act, but not the 1975 Act, extends to local authority sites that would be within this definition were they not exempt from the licensing requirements.

(3) *Does the occupier occupy the caravan as his residence, and* (for the 1975 Act only) *as his only or main residence?* (1968 Act, s 1 (1); 1975 Act, s 1 (1))

B — Rent to be Charged

Only the 1975 Act contains any restriction. On the caravan dweller making a claim, the site owner must offer him a written agreement. That agreement must provide for annual payments (effectively, rent) to be made, with provision for reviews every twelve months (1975 Act, s 3 *(d)*). Disputes can be referred to the county court (1975 Act, s 4 (5), (6)). The court can therefore be called upon to adjudicate upon the initial rent, or a subsequent review, and can backdate the rent (*Grant* v *Allen* [1980] 1 All ER 720). There is, however, no indication of the standards that it should apply.

C — Security of Tenure

1 Period of agreement

The agreement which a caravan dweller is entitled, under the 1975 Act, to claim from the site owner must normally last for at least five years, with an option for the caravan dweller to extend it for a further three (1975 Act, ss 2, 3 *(c)*). The court has no jurisdiction to order a longer period (*Taylor* v *Calvert* [1978] 1 WLR 899). The only exception is where the duration of the site licence or the site owner's own tenure does not extend that long. If in such a case the owner receives an extension, the length of the occupier's agreement must be extended up to the standard period.

Notwithstanding the length of the agreement, the occupier may still bring it to an end by not less than twenty-eight days' written notice.

2 Notice

A notice to terminate an agreement to occupy a caravan or

station one on a caravan site must be given at least four weeks before it takes effect (1968 Act, s 2).

3 Suspension of eviction order

An eviction order made in favour of a caravan site owner after the expiry of a contract giving a right to reside in a caravan, or station a caravan on a site for residential purposes, can be suspended for up to twelve months as the court thinks reasonable (1968 Act, s 4). The court may order a suspension on terms, including as to payment of rent, and either party can subsequently apply for the period to be varied. When suspending a possession order, the court may only make an order for costs if, because of the conduct of either party, there are special reasons for doing so.

In considering whether a possession order should be suspended, the court must take account of all the circumstances, and in particular:

(a) whether the occupier has failed to comply with any terms of the contract or site licence, or reasonable rules for the conduct of the site or maintenance of the caravan;

(b) whether the occupier has unreasonably refused an offer to renew his contract for a reasonable period on reasonable terms;

(c) whether the occupier has failed to make reasonable efforts to secure alternative accommodation for the caravan, or another caravan and accommodation for it, as the case may be.

There is no power to suspend a possession order granted to a local authority.

Chapter XV
Additional Protection for Tenants

Statutes referred to in this chapter:
Rent (Agriculture) Act 1976: '1976 Act.'
Rent Act 1977: '1977 Act.'
Housing Act 1980: '1980 Act.'

A — PREMIUMS

The obvious evasion of rent control, by taking a capital sum from tenants in addition to rent, is countered by making premiums illegal. The legislation is something of an overlapping patchwork, having been enacted piecemeal. There are also certain exceptions to the general rules, when premiums are legal.

1 Meaning of premium

'Premium' is defined by statute as including any fine or other like sum, any other pecuniary consideration in addition to rent, and any deposit unless it does not exceed one-sixth of the annual rent and is reasonable in relation to the liability it is intended to cover (1977 Act, s 128 (1); 1980 Act, s 79).

2 Illegal premiums

No one may, as a condition of the grant, renewal, continuance or assignment of a protected tenancy, require in addition to the rent the payment of any premium or the making of any loan (1977 Act, ss 119, 120 (1), (2)). Payment to a third party is equally forbidden, eg, where a tenant surrenders his lease to the landlord, who grants a new lease to someone who pays a premium to the outgoing tenant (*Farrell* v *Alexander* [1977] AC 59). Contravention is an offence punishable by a fine of up to £100. Anyone receiving any premium is also guilty of an offence. In either case, the convicting court may order repayment of the premium. On the other hand, payments in consideration of the surrender of a protected tenancy are not forbidden.

Where a rent payable under a restricted contract has been registered by a rent tribunal anyone who, as a condition of the grant, renewal, continuance or assignment of rights under such a contract, requires payment of a premium is guilty of an offence (1977 Act, s 122). The penalty is a fine of up to £100 and the court can order the repayment of the premium. This does not prevent anyone requiring the payment of outgoings, or a reasonable amount for goodwill transferred.

An excessive price required for furniture (including fittings and other articles: 1977 Act, s 128 (1)) constitutes a premium (1977 Act, s 123). To offer furniture at an unreasonably high price, or to fail to furnish with particulars of the tenancy an inventory of furniture with each item priced, is also an offence subject to a fine of up to £100, if done in connection with the grant, renewal, continuance or assignment of a protected tenancy (1977 Act, s 124).

Any illegal premium is recoverable by the payer (1977 Act, s 125). If it took the form of a loan, it is repayable on demand.

3 Legal premiums

There will have been cases where a tenant legally paid a premium in respect of a tenancy which only at a later date became subject to the Rent Act. To cope with the injustice which would result if such tenants found that, as soon as the Rent Act applied, they could recover nothing of what they had paid, there are certain exceptions. In these exceptional cases, a premium can legally be paid on assignments (although not on the grant of a new tenancy).

There are two formulae for calculating permitted premiums: one is general, and the other applies to higher value regulated tenancies. The two formulae may yield different results, and in a case to which both apply, the higher resulting figure is permitted (1977 Act, Sched 18, para 6 (1)).

(a) General

This exception applies if the answer to the following three questions is Yes (1977 Act, Sched 18, Pt I):

(1) *Did the tenant lawfully pay a premium (disregarding payments for outgoings) for the grant, continuance or renewal of a regulated tenancy?*

(2) *Is the same tenancy still subsisting, or if not, was any new tenancy granted to the person entitled to possession of the premises immediately before the new tenancy begun?*

(3) *Is a rent registered which (together with any rates paid by the landlord or a superior landlord) is higher than the rent contractually payable?*

The amount of premium that may be charged is calculated with this formula:

$$\frac{P \times A}{G}$$

Where *P* is whichever is the *lesser* of:
    (a) the premium paid; or
    (b) the difference between the registered rent and the contractual rent for the period from the payment of the premium to 'the relevant date'. This last is the end of the term, or any earlier date on which the landlord could terminate it, but with a maximum of seven years.

Where *A* is the period from the date of the assignment to the relevant date.

Where *G* is the period from the date of the grant, continuance or renewal for which the premium was paid, to the relevant date.

The effect of this is to restrict the amount of premium to a proportion on a time basis of the amount originally paid. It will, however, be less if the tenancy had more than seven years to run when the original premium was paid, or if that premium was more than the aggregate of the difference between the registered rent and the contractual rent over the whole period of the tenancy.

(b) Higher value regulated tenancies

This exception applies where the tenant lawfully paid a premium on the grant, renewal or continuance of a higher value regulated tenancy (1977 Act, s 121, Sched 18, Pt II). In this case, the permitted premium is the following fraction of the last premium so paid:

$$\frac{X}{Y}$$

Where X is what remains of the term when the assignment takes place.

Where Y is the whole term.

The term is assumed to expire on the earliest date on which a tenant's notice to terminate it could take effect.

Where a premium was lawfully paid on the grant or assignment of a previous tenancy which was subsequently surrendered, what is called the 'surrender value' of that previous tenancy can be treated as, or, as the case may be, added to, the former premium from which the new permitted premium is calculated. That surrender value is the sum that, at the date of the surrender of the former tenancy, would have been the premium then lawfully chargeable on an assignment under these provisions, had they then applied to it.

4 Long tenancies

Notwithstanding the rules outlined above, premiums are permitted on dealings with tenancies originally granted for over twenty-one years, whether or not subsequently extended by act of the parties or by statute (Landlord and Tenant Act 1954, s 2 (4); 1977 Act, s 127; 1980 Act, s 78 (4)). There are two classes of case: in one premiums are freely chargeable, and in the other limited premiums are allowed.

(a) Premiums freely allowed

There are two alternative sets of conditions for a lease to satisfy which allow premiums to be charged in any circumstances, whether on a grant or assignment.

EITHER, the answer to the following four questions is Yes:

(1) *Was the lease granted before 16 July 1980?*

(2) *Was a premium lawfully required and paid when it was granted?*

(3) *Was the rent then a low rent?*

(4) *Are the lease terms free from an inhibition (defined below) against either assignment or sub-letting, or both?*

OR the answer to the following three questions is Yes:

(1) *Is it beyond the power of the landlord unilaterally to terminate the tenancy within twenty years of its being granted?*

(2) *Are the sums payable by the tenant (excluding any for rates, services, repairs, maintenance and insurance) fixed for at least six (twenty) years from the date the tenancy was granted and thereafter not variable more frequently than every seven (twenty-one) years?*

The shorter periods of years only apply to a lease which was granted after 15 July 1980 at a low rent and which also includes an express limit on rent. The limit is that what the tenant pays (with the same exclusions as in the question) cannot be varied so as to exceed two-thirds of the rateable value of the premises at the date of variation.

This condition does not apply to tenancies granted before 25 July 1969, nor to extended tenancies granted under the Leasehold Reform Act 1967. In the case of a sub-tenancy, one variation within its first twenty years is allowed, provided the condition is satisfied in the case of a superior tenancy.

(3) *Are the terms of the tenancy free from an inhibition against either assignment or sub-letting, or both?* (1980 Act, s 78 (1)–(3)

For this purpose, an inhibition against a form of dealing with the tenancy is a term that precludes it, permits it subject to consent but excludes s 144 of the Law of Property Act 1925 (thereby allowing the landlord to require a payment from the tenant), or permits it subject to consent but requires the tenant to make an offer to surrender.

(b) Limited premiums allowed

In any other case, a proportion of the premium, or last

premium, lawfully paid on the grant or assignment of the tenancy may be charged (1977 Act, s 127 (1) *(b)*, Sched 18, Pt II). The proportion is calculated as for higher value regulated tenancies. When the last premium is paid on an assignment, the period then unexpired of the term is substituted, in the calculation, for the term for which the tenancy was granted.

5 Duchy and Crown estate tenancies

Whether there are any restrictions on premiums on the assignment of a tenancy of which the landlord is the Duchy of Lancaster, the Duchy of Cornwall or the Crown Estate Commissioners and which was made a regulated tenancy by the 1980 Act, depends on the terms of the tenancy (1980 Act, Sched 8, para 4).

If the tenancy was granted for a term certain, and its provisions do not inhibit both assignment and sub-letting the whole premises (within the meaning of question (3), p 109), there is no restriction on the premium that may be lawfully charged on an assignment before the end of the year 1990 if the tenancy also falls into one of two classes. Either, it was an existing tenancy that the 1980 Act made into a regulated tenancy, or it is a regulated tenancy granted to someone then a tenant under a tenancy made regulated by the 1980 Act, or under another tenancy in this class.

In other cases, the restrictions that apply are the same as those affecting higher value regulated tenancies.

B — Security of Tenure

1 Eviction by court order only

Tenants of residential accommodation may not be evicted without a court order. This applies both on the exercise of a right of re-entry or forfeiture and, where they do not enjoy other statutory protection, at the end of their tenancies (Protection from Eviction Act 1977, ss 2, 3). A licensee under a restricted contract also has this protection when the contract ends (Protection from Eviction Act 1977, s 3 (2A); 1980 Act, s 69 (1)). This requirement of proceedings at the end of a tenancy does not extend to tenants under protected tenancies, the control relating to long tenancies, protected occupancies and statutory tenancies under the 1976 Act, mixed business and residential tenancies and lettings of agricultural holdings (Protection from Eviction Act 1977, s 8 (1)). Other statutory provisions will normally require proceedings to be taken in those cases.

Those who have exclusive possession of premises under the terms of their employment, but are not tenants, also have the benefit of this protection (Protection from Eviction Act 1977, s 8 (2)). 'Tenant' and 'tenancy' bear an extended meaning accordingly. Furthermore, not only the tenant is protected, but also anyone lawfully residing in any part of the premises at the termination of the former tenancy, whether contractual or statutory (Protection from Eviction Act 1977, s 3 (2)).

Illegally to deprive an occupier of his occupation, or to attempt to, is an offence (see 'Protection from harassment' below). An injunction may be granted for the redelivery of possession to an occupier illegally deprived of it (*Warder* v *Cooper* [1970] Ch 495).

There are certain exceptions to the rule that an order for possession must be obtained, and these are set out below. The appropriate court is the county court for premises within their limit of jurisdiction for actions for the recovery of land, and the High Court in other cases (Protection from Eviction Act 1977, s 9 (1)–(3)). This does not, however, affect the jurisdiction of the High Court to deal with cases enforcing a lessor's right of re-entry or forfeiture, or by a mortgagee where the former tenancy was not binding on him.

The obligation to apply for a possession order before eviction extends to the Crown (Protection from Eviction Act 1977, s 10).

Exceptions to the requirement that a possession order must be obtained from the county court or the High Court before eviction are (Protection from Eviction Act 1977, s 9 (4)):

(*a*) obtaining possession under a magistrate's warrant of a parsonage house (Pluralities Act 1838, s 59);

(*b*) obtaining possession by magistrates of premises acquired for defence purposes (Defence Act 1842, s 19);

(*c*) obtaining possession under a magistrate's warrant of premises occupied by a person formerly employed in certain ecclesiastical offices (Lecturers and Parish Clerks Act 1844, s 6);

(d) obtaining possession of premises compulsorily acquired under the warrant of the acquiring authority (Compulsory Purchase Act 1965, s 13); and

(e) obtaining possession of premises by order of the court that convicted the tenant of knowingly permitting them to be used as a brothel, where the tenant failed on being so required by the landlord to assign them within three months (Sexual Offences Act 1956, Sched 1, para 3).

2 Protection from harassment

Anyone unlawfully depriving an occupier of his occupation, or attempting to do so, commits an offence (see next section). It is a defence to prove that the accused believed, with reasonable cause, that the occupier had ceased to reside in the premises (Protection from Eviction Act, 1977, s 1 (2)).

Anyone doing acts calculated to interfere with the peace or comfort of the occupier of residential premises or members of his household commits an offence (see next section). 'Premises' need not be more than one room (*Thurrock UDC* v *Shina* (1972) 23 P & CR 205). The act must be done with intent to cause the occupier to give up occupation of all or part of the premises or to refrain from exercising or pursuing any right or remedy in respect thereof (Protection from Eviction Act 1977, s 1 (3)). If, with the same intent, anyone persistently withdraws or withholds services reasonably required for the occupation of the premises as a residence, he also commits an offence. The persistence is a necessary element of the latter offence (*R* v *Abrol* (1972) 116 SJ 177).

For this purpose 'occupier' includes an occupier of all or part of the premises as a residence under any contract (which includes a tenancy, licence or service agreement) and any form of statutory tenancy (Protection from Eviction Act 1977, s 1 (1)).

These criminal proceedings do not prejudice any possible civil liability that the offender may have (Protection from Eviction Act 1977, s 1 (5)). But no civil liability results merely from contravening these statutory provisions (*McCall* v *Abelesz*

[1976] QB 585).

A similar offence is created to prevent the harassment of caravan dwellers by the Caravan Sites Act 1968, s 3, although action-under the Protection from Eviction Act 1977 may sometimes be appropriate (*Norton* v *Knowles* [1969] 1 QB 572).

3 Offences

Offenders in cases other than those relating to caravans are liable on summary conviction to a fine of up to £400, or imprisonment for up to six months, or both. On conviction on indictment, they are liable to a fine, or imprisonment for up to two years, or both. Offenders in caravan cases are liable on summary conviction to a fine of up to £100 for the first offence and up to £500 for the second and subsequent convictions, or to imprisonment for up to six months, or both (Protection from Eviction Act 1977, s 1 (4); Caravan Sites Act 1968, s 3 (3)). Any director, manager, secretary or similar officer of a corporation which has committed an offence or anyone purporting to act in that capacity may also be guilty. If it is proved that the offence was committed with his consent or connivance or was attributable to his neglect, he is liable to the same penalties as the corporation (Protection from Eviction Act 1977, s 1 (6)); Caravan Sites Act 1968, s 14.

The landlord's agent or rent collector may, for the purpose of proceedings, be required to disclose the landlord's full name and place of abode or business, and is subject to a fine of up to £25 on default, unless he did not know, and could not have known, the information (1977 Act, s 151 (3), (4)). Failure by a person receiving or demanding rent for a dwelling, without reasonable excuse, to supply the landlord's name and address within twenty-one days of a written request by the tenant, is an offence carrying a fine of up to £200 (Housing Act 1974, s 121 (1)).

C — AGRICULTURAL WORKERS

1 Extent of control

There is limited protection from eviction for agricultural workers whose accommodation is not within the 1976 Act (Chapter IX).This protection applies if the answer to the following three questions is Yes.

(1) *Did the tenant occupy the premises under the terms of his employment in agriculture?* (Protection from Eviction Act 1977, s 4 (1))

For the definition of employment in agriculture, see pp 72–3.

(2) *Does the tenant fail to qualify as a statutory tenant under the 1976 Act?*

(3) *Is the tenant either the tenant under the tenancy which has ended, or a relative of that tenant?* (Protection from Eviction Act 1977, s 4 (2))

This protection extends to the former tenant's widow or widower residing with the tenant at his death, or if there was none, any member of his family residing there with him.

2 Security of tenure

Security of tenure is provided merely by a very wide power to postpone or suspend the execution of an order for possession on terms as to payment of rent, reinforced by an obligation to suspend it until six months after tenancy ended (Protection from Eviction Act 1977, s 4 (3)–(6)). In certain cases the court need not suspend the order, even though the six months have not elapsed. These are:

(a) if other suitable accommodation is, or will within that time, be available to the tenant;

(b) that, unless the premises are available for an employee of the landlord, the efficient management of any agricultural land, or the efficient carrying on of an agricultural operation, will be prejudiced;

(c) that the suspension of the order would cause greater hardship (but not in relation to the agricultural business) than its execution;

(d) that the tenant, or someone residing or lodging with him, has damaged the premises or has been guilty of conduct which is a nuisance or annoyance to the occupiers of other premises;

(e) it would not be reasonable to suspend the order for the remainder of the period.

A court that makes a possession order, but suspends it under these provisions, is not to make an order for costs unless, having regard to the conduct of the parties, there are special reasons (Protection from Eviction Act 1977, s 4 (9)). The tenant's failure to seek alternative accommodation may constitute a special reason (*Wilson* v *Croft* [1971] 1 QB 241).

Chapter XVI
Rent Allowances

Statutes referred to in this chapter:
Housing Finance Act 1972: '1972 Act.'
Housing Rents and Subsidies Act 1975: '1975 Act.'
Rent (Agriculture) Act 1976: '1976 Act.'
Rent Act 1977: '1977 Act.'
Housing Act 1980: '1980 Act.'

1 Introduction

The 1972 Act provides a model scheme for rent allowances (cash payments towards rent paid to landlords). A local authority may vary this scheme, but the variations are not to be such that any individual receives a smaller allowance than he would under the model scheme (1972 Act, s 21 (4)), nor may the total allowances paid by the authority in any year exceed by more than 10 per cent what they would have paid under the model scheme (1972 Act, ss 20 (8), 22 (1)).

2 Rent allowance schemes

A copy of the rent allowance scheme is to be available for public inspection free at all reasonable hours at the authority's principal office (1972 Act, s 24 (1)). A copy can be obtained at a reasonable fee. A landlord letting premises must give the tenant written particulars of the rent allowance scheme in that area. These particulars are to include the procedure on making an application for an allowance and the information required, and the circumstances in which an allowance is likely to be given, with examples. These particulars can be obtained free from the local authority by both landlords and tenants. Every rent book issued to a tenant who pays rent weekly must also have these particulars inserted in it. In default, the landlord (other than a county council or the Housing Corporation) is liable to a fine of up to £50 on summary conviction. Where the landlord is a body corporate, any director, manager, secretary or other officer as a result of whose negligence or with whose consent or connivance the offence was committed is jointly liable (1972 Act, s 24 (3), (9)–(14)).

3 Who is eligible: tenants

A tenant can apply for a rent allowance if he can answer Yes to any one of questions (1)–(4), and also Yes to both questions (5) and (6).

In one case, someone other than the tenant may qualify for an allowance. Where the tenant is one spouse, but the premises are occupied by the other spouse who pays the rent, the authority may at their discretion treat the occupier as tenant, giving notice of their decision (1972 Act, Sched 4, para 1 (3)).

(1) *Are the premises let on a regulated tenancy, a restricted contract (including a letting by a resident landlord), an assured tenancy, or a statutory tenancy under the 1976 Act?* (1972 Act, s 19 (5) *(a)*, *(b)*, *(d)*, *(g)*; 1980 Act, Sched 15, para 3)

This only includes a 1976 Act statutory tenancy, where the rent is at least two-thirds of the rateable value on 23 March 1965, or the first day thereafter that the premises were rated.

(2) *Are the premises let on terms that would constitute a restricted contract, but for the fact that the rent includes payment for board?* (1972 Act, s 19 (5) *(c)*; 1980 Act, Sched 15, para 3)

(3) *Are the premises let on a tenancy that would have been regulated, had the landlord not been one of the following bodies?* (1972 Act, s 19 (5) *(e)*, *(f)*, *(7)*; 1980 Act, Sched 15, para 3)

The landlords concerned are:

(a) a county council;

(b) the Housing Corporation;

(c) a housing association. If the tenant, or his personal representative, is entitled to receive a sum calculated directly or indirectly on the value of the premises on ceasing to be a member of the association, he is not eligible;

(d) a housing trust;

(e) a housing co-operative.

(4) *Does the tenant occupy hostel or shared accommodation?*
(1972 Act, s 19 (5) *(h)*, (6); 1980 Act, Sched 15, para 3)

Hostel accommodation is in a building providing residential accommodation which is not in separate and self-contained units. Allowances can be claimed in respect of payments under a licence of hostel accommodation.

Shared accommodation is premises shared in such a way that, for that reason, the letting is excluded from one of the categories for which an allowance would be payable.

(5) *Is the tenant other than a service tenant?* (1972 Act, s 19 (3))

A tenant who occupies premises pursuant to a contract of service which requires that he be provided with a dwelling at a specified rent does not qualify for a rent allowance.

(6) *Is neither the tenant, nor any person with whose income or resources the tenant's fall to be aggregated, receiving supplementary benefit?* (1980 Act, s 119 (1))

4 Who is eligible: almspeople

Those whose home is accommodation in an almshouse provided by a charity, registered under the Charities Act 1960, s 4, or exempt from such registration, can obtain rent allowances (1975 Act, s 12). Almspeople, as the Act calls them, do not pay rent as they are not true tenants. For this purpose, however, the contribution that they pay to the almshouse charity counts as their rent, provided that it does not exceed the maximum for the time being approved by the Charity Commissioners. The Almshouse Contributions (Allowances) (England and Wales) Regulations 1975 adapt the rules about allowances to this special case.

5 Exclusions

A rent allowance may be withheld at the local authority's discretion in two cases (1972 Act, Sched 4, para 13):

     (i) where the landlord resides with the tenant; and

     (ii) where the landlord is a member of the tenant's family,

and it appears that the tenancy was created to take advantage of the allowance scheme.

The other major categories of residential lettings excluded from allowance schemes are those of:

(i) premises whose relevant rateable value exceeds the Rent Act limits;

(ii) mixed residential and business lettings;

(iii) agricultural holdings;

(iv) premises of which the Crown (but not the Crown Estate Commissioners) is landlord;

(v) premises of which a co-ownership housing society is landlord.

6 Procedure

An applicant for a rent allowance must furnish the authority with such written information and evidence as it reasonably requires concerning (1972 Act, Sched 4, para 2 (1)):

(i) the persons residing with the landlord;

(ii) the rent in respect of any premises sub-let;

(iii) his other income and his liquid cash resources, and those of his spouse (which includes a person living as husband or wife although unmarried: 1972 Act, Sched 4, para 1 (4)).

Applicants may also be required to give evidence of (1972 Act, Sched 4, para 12 (1)):

(i) their interest in the premises;

(ii) the rent paid for any relevant period.

This information may be required later, while the allowance is being paid.

The authority must first decide whether the applicant is eligible for an allowance. If he is eligible, the authority must then assess what is likely to be his income, and that of his spouse, during the period for which the allowance will be granted. This period is up to nine months from the date the tenant is notified that his application has been successful, when he is notified during March or April. Otherwise, it is up to seven months. For those of pensionable age, the period can be up to twelve months (1972 Act, Sched 4, paras 3 (1), 4 (2); Rent Rebate and Rent

Allowance Schemes (England and Wales) Regulations 1978, art 2).

On coming to a decision, the authority must notify the tenant in writing (1972 Act, Sched 4, para 15). The tenant is entitled to make representations concerning the determination to the authority within one month, and these must be considered by the authority, who may alter or confirm their decision according to the circumstances, and must notify the tenant in writing with reasons. An application can be withdrawn at any time, whereupon the authority need do no more about it (1972 Act, Sched 4, para 2 (3)).

An allowance is payable from the beginning of the rental period in which the application was received (1972 Act, Sched 4, para 4 (1)). A further allowance may be granted to start when the first finishes if the tenant applies at least one month before the first period expires (1972 Act, Sched 4, para 10). If the renewal application is made late, the new allowance starts from the rental period during which the application is made. In exceptional circumstances, the first allowance can be back-dated for up to twelve months, and a renewal can be back-dated so that the continuity of payment is unbroken (Rent Rebate and Rent Allowance Schemes (England) Regulations 1974, art 4; Rent Rebate and Rent Allowance Schemes (Wales) Regulations 1974, art 4; Rent Rebate and Rent Allowances Schemes (England and Wales) (No 2) Regulations 1978, art 7).

The authority may pay the allowance at such times and in such manner as they think fit (1972 Act, Sched 4, para 1 (1)). They must have regard to the reasonable needs and convenience of the tenant (1972 Act, Sched 4, para 12 (2), (3) (b)), but if they are not satisfied that he is paying his rent, they may pay the allowance direct to the landlord.

Where the tenant's circumstances change and he is in receipt of an allowance, or the authority's scheme is amended altering his entitlement, they may adjust the allowance or end it as necessary, inviting the tenant to submit a new application as appropriate (1972 Act, Sched 4, paras 6–8). The authority have no duty to make an alteration where the result is that the tenant's entitlement rises or falls by less than the minimum allowance payable under the authority's scheme.

7 Amount payable

The explanations, calculations and illustrations in this section all relate to the model scheme set out in the 1972 Act, which individual authorities are empowered to modify.

(a) The calculation formula

Rent allowances *(RA)* are calculated by reference to the following six factors, each of which is examined in detail below:

    (i) the tenant's needs allowance *(na)*;
    (ii) the income of the tenant and his spouse *(inc)*;
    (iii) the amount of the rent *(r)*;
    (iv) a minimum rent *(min)*;
    (v) minimum and maximum allowances;
    (vi) a deduction for non-dependants *(ndd)*.

All these are quoted in weekly amounts, and where they come from figures calculated by reference to any other period, they must be converted to weekly sums (1972 Act, Sched 3, para 3 (1)).

The calculation varies depending upon whether the income is above or below the needs allowance, which is in effect the minimum income level.

If the income *equals or is less than* the needs allowance, the formula is:

  A From the rent deduct the minimum rent;
  B From the balance deduct the non-dependants deduction;
  C The result is the allowance, provided it exceeds the minimum and to the extent that.it is not greater than the maximum.

This may be expressed as:

$r - min - ndd = RA$.

If the income is *greater than* the needs allowance, the formula is:

  A From the income deduct the needs allowance;
  B Take 17 per cent of the result;
  C Add the minimum rent to that figure;
  D Deduct the result from the rent;
  E From the balance deduct the non-dependants deduction;
  F The result is the allowance, provided it exceeds the

minimum and to the extent that it is not greater than the maximum.

This may be expressed as:

$$r - \frac{17\,(inc\,-\,na)}{100} + min - ndd = RA$$

(b) Needs allowance

There are two scales of needs allowance, a standard one and a higher one for substantially and permanently handicapped people (registered under National Assistance Act 1948, s 29 (1), as extended by Chronically Sick and Disabled Persons Act 1970, s 2). The rates are (Rent Rebate and Rent Allowance Schemes (and Services Amendment) (England and Wales) Regulations 1979, art 6):

	Standard rate	Handicapped people
Individual person		
with no dependent child	£31.05	£34.60
with dependent child(ren)	£45.55	£49.10
Married couple	£45.55	—
of whom one handicapped	—	£49.10
both handicapped	—	£50.80
Each dependent child, add	£7.70	£7.70

(c) Income

The income of the tenant and his spouse must be aggregated (1972 Act, Sched 4, para 3 (1)). For this purpose the spouse is the person with whom the tenant lives, even if they are not married, and not a legal spouse from whom he or she is separated. Two or more joint tenants may be treated as a sole tenant (1972 Act, Sched 3, para 4 (1)). If anyone residing with the tenant has a higher income than he, the authority may treat that other person as the tenant if they think it reasonable, in which case they must give notice of that decision (1972 Act, Sched 3, para 5 (1)). In this section, the relevant person or people are for simplicity referred to as the tenant.

The first calculation is of a gross income for the allowance period. In so far as it consists of earnings from a gainful occupation, the estimate is based on the gross earnings either for the five weeks ending with the last pay day before the application was made where payment is weekly, or for the last two months if paid monthly, unless some other period seems appropriate to the authority (1972 Act, Sched 4, para (2), (3)). If earnings are not paid by regular sums (eg, where the tenant is self-employed), the figure to be taken is the net profit after deduction of expenses but before payment of income tax and the tenant's own national insurance contribution, estimated on such basis as seems appropriate in each case (1972 Act, Sched 4, para 3 (6)). The Secretary of State has given directions for the treatment of statutory tax-free payments set out in Department of the Environment Circular 74/72. Any maintenance payments to a dependent child under sixteen are added (Rent Rebate and Rent Allowance Schemes (and Services Amendment) (England and Wales) Regulations 1979, art 5 *(a)*).

Any of the following adjustments that are appropriate must be made to the gross income (Rent Rebate and Rent Allowance Schemes (England and Wales) (No 3) Regulations 1975, art 4); Rent Rebate and Rent Allowance Schemes (England and Wales) Regulations 1976, art 4; Rent Rebate and Rent Allowance Schemes (and Services Amendment) (England and Wales) Regulations 1979, art 5).

The gross income must be *reduced* by:

(i) rent received from a sub-tenant other than for furniture or services;

(ii) payments received from a dependent child or a non-dependant;

(iii) £5 of the tenant's earnings and £5 of those of his spouse;

(iv) any grants for education;

(v) attendance allowances (as defined for the purposes of the Family Income Supplements Act 1970);

(vi) sums payable to the holders of the Victoria Cross and the George Cross;

(vii) benefits payable under the Supplementary Benefit Act 1976;

(viii) where the tenant is a 'qualifying student', £10 (Rent Rebates and Rent Allowances (Students) (England and

Wales) Regulations 1980, art 2), and any sum by which his grant is increased for the maintenance of a home elsewhere than his place of residence during his course.

Qualifying students are those in receipt of grants or awards under the Education Act 1962, ss 1–3, for attendance at courses designated by or under the State Award Regulations 1963, or state studentships, or awards of grants determined by the Secretary of State to be analogous (Rent Rebates and Rent Allowances (Students) (England and Wales) Regulations 1976, art 2 (2)).

A maximum of £4 in respect of the following:

(ix) £4 of :

(a) a war disablement pension (as defined for the purposes of the Family Income Supplements Act 1970);

(b) industrial disablement benefit (being a weekly payment under the Social Security Act 1975);

(c) an old cases allowance (weekly payments under a scheme pursuant to the Industrial Injuries and Diseases (Old Cases) Act 1975);

(d) any payment that the Secretary of State accepts as being analogous;

(x) £4 of that part of the following that exceeds the rate for a contributory widow's pension under the Social Security Act 1975, Sched 4:

(a) a widow's pension by way of industrial injuries benefit under the Social Security Act 1975, s 68;

(b) a widow's pension (excluding any allowance for children) granted for death due to service or war injury under, or pursuant to schemes made under, Ministry of Pensions Act 1916, Air Force (Constitution) Act 1917, Personal Injuries (Emergency Provisions) Act 1939, Pensions (Navy, Army, Air Force and Mercantile Marine) Act 1939, Polish Resettlement Act 1947, Home Guard Act 1951, Ulster Defence Regiment Act 1969, Injuries in War (Compensation) Acts 1914 and 1914 (Session 2), or any War Risk Compensation Scheme for the Mercantile Marine (Rent Rebate and Rent Allowance Schemes (England and Wales) Regulations 1977, art 4);

(*c*) any payment that the Secretary of State accepts as being analogous;

(xi) £4 of the total of all charitable payments and voluntary payments by a non-dependant for the maintenance of his spouse (even if living apart), former spouse or children;

(xii) any maintenance payments by the tenant or his spouse to a former spouse, or to children other than dependent children.

(*d*) *Rent*

In calculating a rent allowance various adjustments must be made to the rent actually paid, if they are applicable. Sums attributable to rates, furniture and services are disregarded (1972 Act, s 25 (1)–(5)).

The authority must reduce the amount of the rent taken into account by what they consider reasonable in all the circumstances if (1972 Act, Sched 3, para 16):

(i) they consider that the tenant occupies premises larger than he reasonably requires; or

(ii) they consider that his rent is exceptionally high, compared with other comparable private tenancies in their area, because of the location of the premises.

If the tenant is a 'qualifying student' (p 124), the amount of his rent eligible for an allowance is reduced by £10 (Rent Rebates and Rent Allowances (Students) (England and Wales) Regulations 1980, art 2).

The authority must also disregard any rent in excess of any of the following limits (1972 Act, Sched 4, paras 14, 14A; 1976 Act, Sched 7, para 5):

(i) the registered or recoverable rent for a regulated tenancy, or if none is registered, the authority's estimate of the fair rent;

(ii) the registered rent for lettings by housing associations, housing trusts and the Housing Corporation or, if none, the authority's estimate of the fair rent;

(iii) the registered rent for a statutory tenancy of an agricultural tied cottage, or if none, the authority's estimate of the fair rent;

(iv) the conditions imposed on the letting of grant-aided accommodation for farmworkers, on the letting of houses sold by a local authority and on the letting of premises containing improvements aided by a grant under the Housing (Financial Provisions) Act 1958, s 33, as extended by the House Purchase and Housing Act 1959.

If a tenant is paid a rent allowance based on a rent over those limits and he is entitled to recover the excess rent, the authority can recover from him the amount by which that excess rent increased his allowance.

(e) Minimum weekly rent

The minimum weekly rent varies according to whether the tenant's income comes up to his needs allowance (1972 Act, Sched 3, para 10). It is generally 40 per cent of the actual weekly rent (as adjusted) or £1, whichever is greater. If, however, the tenant's income is less than his needs allowance, that figure is reduced by 25 per cent of the difference between his income and the needs allowance.

(f) Minimum and maximum allowances

The minimum allowance is 20p per week (1972 Act, Sched 3, para 13). If in any particular case the calculations throw up a smaller figure nothing is payable.

The maximum allowance is £25 for premises in Greater London and £23 for those elsewhere (1972 Act, Sched 3, para 14; Rent Rebate and Rent Allowance Schemes (England and Wales) Regulations 1980, art 3).

(g) Non-dependants deduction

The non-dependants that have to be taken into account are all the adults who live in the premises that the tenant occupies except (1972 Act, Sched 3, para 2 (1)):

(i) the tenant himself;

(ii) the tenant's spouse (which extends to include those living as husband and wife even if not married);

(iii) dependent children of the tenant or his spouse;

(iv) a joint tenant who is treated together with one or more other joint tenants as sole tenant;

(v) a person with higher income than the tenant whom the authority choose to treat as the tenant.

The deductions for each non-dependant are (1972 Act, Sched 3, para 12; Rent Rebate and Rent Allowance Schemes (and Services Amendment) (England and Wales) Regulations 1979, art 6):

(i) Those not in receipt of supplementary benefit and not undergoing full-time instruction:

If between 18 and 21 years	£1.85
If over 21 and under pensionable age	£2.80
If of pensionable age (unless a couple living together)	£1.10
If a couple of pensionable age	£1.10

(ii) Qualifying students (defined: p 124):

If between 18 and 21 years	£1.85
If over 21 and under pensionable age	£2.80

(iii) Those in receipt of supplementary benefit (a married couple for both of whom benefit is paid, treated as one person) £1.10

Chapter XVII
Enfranchisement and Extended Leases: General

Statutes referred to in this chapter:
Leasehold Property (Temporary Provisions) Act 1951: '1951 Act.'
Landlord and Tenant Act 1954: '1954 Act.'
Leasehold Reform Act 1967: '1967 Act.'
Housing Act 1974: '1974 Act.'
Rent (Agriculture) Act 1976: '1976 Act.'
Housing Act 1980: '1980 Act.'

Regulations referred to in this chapter:
The Leasehold Reform (Enfranchisement and Extension) Regulations 1967: 'Regs'

A — CLAIMS TO EXERCISE RIGHTS

1 Qualifications to claim rights

A notice claiming enfranchisement or an extended lease may be served when all the following ten questions are answered Yes.

(1) *Do the premises consist of a house?*

For this purpose a house includes any building designed or adapted for living in and reasonably called a house (1967 Act, s 2 (1), (2)). It need not be detached, nor solely designed or adapted for living in. A building originally designed as a dwelling-house, part of which had for some time been used for business purposes for which there had been physical alterations, including the installation of a shop front, was held to be a house for this purpose (*Lake* v *Bennett* [1970] 1 QB 663). It may be divided horizontally into flats and maisonettes, but if it is, the individual sub-divisions are not separate houses, even though the whole building may qualify as a house. The tenant does not enjoy the statutory rights where any material part of the house lies above or below any part of the structure and to which it is attached, and which is not part of the house, or which, in order to bring the house within the rateable value limit, the tenant voluntarily excludes from his application (*Parsons* v *Trustees of Henry Smith's Charity* [1974] 1 WLR 435). Where a building is divided vertically, each sub-division may be a house for this purpose, but the whole cannot be.

The result of this is that the leaseholder of a single flat cannot enfranchise or claim an extended lease. If, however, he is tenant of the whole building, but he has sub-let the other flats he enjoys the rights if the building as a whole can reasonably be called a house. This is intended to include conversions but exclude 'purpose-built' blocks of flats.

On the other hand, the tenant of a semi-detached or terrace house cannot include adjoining houses in his claim, even if they are included in his lease. But an opening made between two adjoining houses will not necessarily preclude enfranchisement of one of them (*Wolf* v *Crutchley* [1971] 1 WLR 99).

(2) *Does the rateable value of the house fall within the following limits?* (1967 Act, s 1 (1) *(a)*; 1974 Act, s 118 (1))

To judge whether a house falls within the rateable value limits, three factors have to be considered: 'the appropriate day', which is 23 March 1965, or the first day thereafter when the house was rated; the date of the grant of the long lease under which the tenant claims; and whether the house is in Greater London.

The rateable value limits are as follows on p 130, judged on the appropriate day (1967 Act, s 1(4)), except in the cases marked *, when the value on 1 April 1973 is taken.

These provisions extend the scope of the right to enfranchise and to claim an extended lease, as originally the rateable value limits on the appropriate day were £400 in Greater London and £200 elsewhere. Some special rules apply to the cases qualifying only because of the extension of rateable value limits. They are referred to in this book as '1974 cases'.

	Appropriate day before 1 April 1973		Appropriate day on or after 1 April 1973	
	Greater London	*Elsewhere*	*Greater London*	*Elsewhere*
Lease granted before 19 Feb 1966	£1,500* If limits below were exceeded.	£750*	£1,500	£750
Lease granted after 18 Feb 1966	£400	£200	£1,000	£500

A house may fall outside the rateable value limits merely because improvements made or paid for by the tenant, or a previous tenant, had the effect of increasing the re-assessment of rateable value that took effect on 1 April 1973. In such a case, the tenant may claim to have the rateable value deemed to be reduced, for this purpose only (1974 Act, s 118 (3), Sched 8). Only improvements effected by works of structural alteration (including installing central heating: *Pearlman* v *Keepers and Governors of Harrow School* [1979] QB 56), extension or addition may be taken into account.

The tenant must serve notice on the landlord in the prescribed form. This sets out the improvements concerned and requires the landlord to agree a reduction in the rateable value for this purpose. Landlord and tenant may at any time agree the reduction in writing. In default of agreement on any of the following questions, within six weeks of service of the notice on the landlord, the county court may determine them: whether the improvement is eligible; what works were involved; whether the tenant or a previous tenant made, or contributed to, it; what proportion the contribution was to the whole cost. Application to the court must be made between six and twelve weeks after the service of notice on the landlord, unless the court grants an extension.

If within two weeks of those factual questions being agreed or determined, the parties have not agreed in writing what reduction in the rateable value is appropriate, the tenant has a further four weeks to apply to the valuation officer for his certificate of the appropriate reduction. A further form is prescribed for that application.

The tenant is liable to bear the landlord's reasonable costs of investigating any matter specified in a notice claiming a reduction in the rateable value served on or after 21 December 1979 (1980 Act, Sched 21, para 8 *(d)*).

(3) *Is the tenant occupying under one of the following two types of tenancy:*

(a) a tenancy granted for a term certain exceeding twenty-one years ('long tenancy')? (1967 Act, s 3 (1))

In deciding the length of the original letting, the possibility of premature determination by re-entry, forfeiture or the exercise of an option to determine must be ignored. The twenty-one years must run from the date of the grant of the lease, even though the habendum is back-dated (*Roberts* v *Church Commissioners for England* [1972] 1 QB 278). A perpetually renewable tenancy is included, unless it is a sub-tenancy and the head tenancy is not a long tenancy. A tenancy terminable on notice after a death or marriage does not qualify if granted before 18 April 1980 (1980 Act, Sched 21, para 3). Such a lease granted on or after that date, unless pursuant to a contract made before that date, is a long lease unless it satisfies three conditions. They are: first, that it is the tenant's death or marriage after which notice may be given; secondly, that the length of the notice cannot exceed three months; and thirdly, that the terms of the lease exclude both the assignment and the sub-letting of the whole of the demised premises.

In one special case, the term 'long tenancy' also includes a lease originally granted for less than twenty-one years. This is where it contains an obligation to renew without payment of premium (but not so that it was perpetually renewable), and it has been renewed so that the total of the terms exceeds twenty-one years (1967 Act, s 3 (4)).

(b) a tenancy, other than a tenancy at will, which arose on the termination of a long tenancy at a low rent (see next question)? (1967 Act, s 3 (2))

A long tenancy includes any extension of one under the 1951 Act or under Pt I or Pt II of the 1954 Act (1967 Act, s 3 (5)). The later tenancy, which is not a long tenancy in its own right, must be granted to the tenant under the long tenancy at the date it ended. However, once the later tenancy has been deemed to be a long tenancy, the benefit enures not only to the original tenant, but also to his assignees (*Austin* v *Dick Richards Properties Ltd* [1975] 1 WLR 1033).

(4) *Is the rent when the tenant serves his notice less than two-thirds of the rateable value of the premises on whichever is the latest of : 23 March 1965, the first day that the premises appeared on the valuation list and the first day of the tenancy?* (1967 Act, s 4 (1))

This is what the 1967 Act refers to as a 'low rent'. Only the rent proper, and not insurance rent or payments for repairs, maintenance or services reserved as rent, is counted. If the rent has been reduced under the terms of the tenancy because the premises were damaged, the reduction is to be ignored. Similarly, any penal addition to the rent because of a breach of the terms of the tenancy is ignored.

The rent and rateable value of the whole house must be compared, but any adjustments to the extent of the premises included in the letting for the purposes of the notice are ignored (1967 Act, s 4 (2), (4), (6)). If a single rent covers other premises as well, an apportionment must be made according to the circumstances. In default of agreement, this apportionment is determined by the county court, or, by agreement or in a case where other matters have been referred to it, by the leasehold valuation tribunal (1967 Act, ss 20 (3), 21 (2) *(b)*; 1980 Act, Sched 22, para 8 (3)).

Although under two-thirds of the rateable value, the rent on a letting (other than a building lease) between 1 September 1939, and 31 March 1963 (inclusive) is not a 'low rent' if it initially exceeded two-thirds of the property's then letting value on the terms of the tenancy. That letting value cannot exceed the legally recoverable rent under the then current rent restriction legislation (*Gidlow-Jackson* v *Middlegate Properties Ltd* [1974] QB 361).

(5) *During the period of three years before the tenant gives notice, or periods amounting to three out of the previous ten years, did the tenant occupy the house as his only or main residence, either as a tenant under a long tenancy at a low rent, or while the tenant under such a tenancy was a member of his family to whom he succeeded?* (1967 Act, ss 1 (1), (2), 7 (1); 1980 Act, Sched 21, para 1)

The fact that the tenant only occupies part of the premises let to him, or has sub-let part which is occupied by someone else, does not disqualify him (1967 Act, s 1 (2) *(a)*; *Harris* v *Swick Securities Ltd* [1969] 1 WLR 1604). No residence by a corporation (including a corporation sole) can count for this purpose (1967 Act, s 37 (5)). Regularly sleeping in a house is not conclusive proof that it is the tenant's only or main residence (*Byrne* v *Rowbotham* (1969) 210 EG 823), and there are circumstances in which husband and wife can have separate main residences, although not estranged (*Fowell* v *Radford and Others* (1969) 114 SJ 34).

A tenant's occupation of the house as sole tenant for life under the Settled Land Act 1925, or because he was entitled or permitted to occupy it under some other trust, may be counted as his own (1967 Act, s 6 (1)).

Occupation in the following circumstances does not count towards the qualifying three-year period (1967 Act, s 1 (2), *(b)*, (3)):

(*a*) where the tenant occupies the house with other land or premises let therewith, and to which the house is ancillary. So if the house is a subsidiary part of factory premises all let together, occupation of the house does not entitle the tenant to serve notice claiming enfranchisement or an extended lease;

(*b*) where the house is comprised in an agricultural holding for the purposes of the Agricultural Holdings Act 1948;

(*c*) where the only letting is by a mortgagor attorning tenant to a mortgagee or chargee.

A tenant can succeed to the following members of his family: his spouse, his children, his children-in-law and his spouse's children (including illegitimate, adopted and step-children), his parents and his parents-in-law (1967 Act, s 7 (7)). A number of tenants' periods of occupation can be added together if each is counted as a relative of the one before, even if they do not all count as members of the family of the eventual claimant (1967 Act, s 7 (1) *(b)*). For example, a grandson may, if necessary, count periods during which the tenant was his father (who is a member of his family for this purpose) and his grandfather (who is not, but is a member of his father's family).

A tenant succeeds to the tenancy of the house for this purpose where it vests in him or his personal representative (1967 Act, s 7 (2)–(6)):

(a) pursuant to a will or the rules of intestacy, other than merely in the capacity of personal representative;

(b) by appropriation in or towards satisfaction of a legacy, share in residue, debt, or other share in or claim upon the estate, or by purchase from the personal representatives during the administration.

Normally, the surviving spouse of an intestate cannot insist upon having the deceased's interest in the matrimonial home as part of his statutory legacy where it is held on a lease terminable within two years of the death (Intestates' Estates Act 1952, Sched 2, para 12 (2)). He is now given that right either if he will then be able to enfranchise or claim an extended lease, or if the deceased spouse had given notice so to do, and the benefit of the notice is appropriated with the tenancy (1967 Act, s 7 (8));

(c) under a settlement, under which the deceased member of the family was sole tenant for life for the purposes of the Settled Land Act 1925, or, in such a case, by appropriation or by purchase from the special or general personal representatives;

(d) under any other form of trust, under which the deceased member of the family was entitled or permitted to occupy the house, or, in such a case, by appropriation or by purchase from the trustees.

In these last two cases, the occupation of the deceased member of the family will count as if he had been the tenant of the house, and as if the provisions of the trust taking effect after his death had been provisions of his will. A person becoming entitled on the termination of a trust has the same rights as if he were entitled under its terms.

Where the house is subject to a settlement, there may not be a tenant in occupation. For such occupation there is substituted the residence of the sole tenant for life under the Settled Land Act 1925, or in any other case that of a beneficiary who is entitled or permitted to occupy. In the last case, the occupation accrues to the benefit of the trustees (1967 Act, s 6).

(6) *Is the notice given:*

(a) before the tenant has given notice terminating his tenancy, and

(b) if a landlord's notice to terminate a long tenancy or a business tenancy has been given under the 1954 Act, s 4 or s 25, not more than two months thereafter? (1967 Act, Sched 3, paras 1, 2)

If a tenant withdraws a notice to enfranchise, he can, with his withdrawal, give notice claiming an extended lease, notwithstanding that the two months have then elapsed. The landlord can agree to waive the two-month limit.

(7) *Has the tenant refrained from requesting a new lease under the 1954 Act, s 26, or from entering into an agreement for a future tenancy under s 28?* (1967 Act, Sched 3, para 1)

(8) *Is the landlord someone other than the Crown, the National Trust (in enfranchisement cases only), or, subject to the conditions mentioned, one of the following public authorities or a tenant deriving title from the Crown?* (1967 Act, ss 28, 32, 33; Development of Rural Wales Act 1976, Sched 7, para 5)

(A) *Public authorities* – The following public authorities can resist a tenant's notice if a Minister of the Crown certifies that they will within ten years require the house for redevelopment, for purposes other than investment:

(a) county, district and London borough councils, the Greater London Council and the Common Council of the City of London, joint boards of local authorities and any combined police authority under the Police Act 1964 (in

the case of local authorities, comprehensive redevelopment of an area suffices, even if it will be carried out by someone else);

(b) the Commission for the New Towns and development corporations for new towns;

(c) the Development Board for Rural Wales;

(d) universities, university colleges, constituent colleges of universities and recognised societies, and colleges incorporated into or schools of London University;

(e) any Regional, Area or special Health Authority (National Health Service Reorganisation Act 1973, Sched 4, para 111);

(f) statutory bodies corporate carrying on a nationalised industry or undertaking;

(g) where they are not included above, harbour authorities under the Harbours Act 1964, and statutory water undertakers under the Water Act 1945, but only so far as they are carrying on those functions;

(g) any other bodies having functions of a public nature included by order of the Secretary of State.

The authority must give the tenant a written notice that the Minister is considering granting a certificate, and that the tenant has twenty-one days in which to make representations (1967 Act, s 28 (4)). The effect of the certificate is two-fold. Once it is issued, a tenant's notice to enfranchise or claiming an extended lease is of no effect. However, when the certificate is served on the tenant he becomes entitled to compensation when the landlord applies for possession, as he would if his landlord claimed possession during an extended lease. This right arises in two circumstances. First, the tenant is entitled when he serves his notice to enfranchise or claiming an extended lease before a copy of the certificate is served on him. Otherwise the tenant must, within two months after service of the copy certificate, give the landlord notice on the prescribed fòrm claiming to be entitled to enfranchise or claim an extended lease (1967 Act, s 28 (1) (b)).

(B) *Crown tenants* – A landlord is himself a Crown tenant for this purpose if any subsisting superior interest in the premises belongs to the Crown Estate, to Her Majesty in right of the

Duchy of Lancaster, to the Duchy of Cornwall or to a government department or is held for its purposes. In only two cases can a tenant enforce his rights to enfranchise or claim an extended lease against a landlord who is a Crown tenant. Where the tenant claims an extended lease and the landlord has a sufficient interest to grant it, and is entitled so to do without Crown authority, then the landlord is in the same position as all other private landlords and must comply. Otherwise, he must comply only if he is notified by (as the case may be) the Crown Estate Commissioners, the Chancellor of the Duchy of Lancaster, a person appointed by the Duke of Cornwall or the Minister in charge of the relevant government department that, as far as the Crown interest is concerned, they will concur in granting the freehold or extended lease.

(9) *Are the premises free from any subsisting notice to treat or contract for sale to a person or body with compulsory purchase powers, whether served on or entered into by the landlord or tenant?* (1967 Act, s 5 (6) *(a)*)

(10) *If the tenant wishes to enfranchise and previously gave a notice to enfranchise the same house which he withdrew, have at least three years elapsed since that withdrawal?* (1967 Act, s 9 (3) *(b)*; 1980 Act, Sched 21, para 1 (2))

2 Extent of premises included

Primarily, the premises to be included in the tenant's claim to enfranchise or for an extended lease are those included in his tenancy and occupied by him. Where the letting of the house included, for occupation with the house, any garage, outhouse, garden, yard and other appurtenances (which cannot include corporeal hereditaments: *Methuen-Campbell* v *Walters* [1979] QB 525), these are included. But garden land let under a separate lease is not included, at least where there was no reasonably close connection between the two transactions (*Gaidowski* v *Gonville and Caius College, Cambridge* [1975] 1 WLR 1066). Certain variations to the extent of the premises may, however, be made on the initiative of the landlord (1967 Act, s 2 (4)). With the tenant's agreement, or on satisfying the court that it is unreasonable to require the landlord to retain them, the landlord may require that premises originally let with the house, but not at the relevant time occupied by the tenant, be included in the claim. The landlord must give the tenant written notice objecting to the further severance of those premises within two months of service of the notice claiming to enfranchise or to have an extended lease.

The premises may be extended to include other premises in which the landlord has an interest when the tenant serves his notice. Within two months the landlord must give written notice to the tenant objecting to their further severance from the house. The additional premises are then included if the tenant agrees, or if the county court is satisfied that it would be unreasonable for the landlord to retain them without the house.

The premises affected may also be reduced. The landlord may object to the inclusion of any part which lies above or below other premises in which he has an interest at the time when the tenant serves his notice. He must give the tenant written notice within two months. That part is then excluded if the tenant agrees, or the county court is satisfied that the difficulties and hardship or inconvenience involved in continued severance outweigh the likely hardship or inconvenience to the tenant resulting from exclusion (but taking into account anything which can be done to mitigate this and any undertaking the landlord gives to take steps to mitigate it).

Mines and minerals beneath the house are excluded if the landlord requires, provided that proper provision is made for support, so that the house can continue to be enjoyed as under the terms of the tenancy.

B — LANDLORD'S GROUNDS FOR OPPOSITION

1 Tenant not entitled

The circumstances in which the tenant is entitled to enfranchise or claim an extended lease are precisely defined. A landlord is entitled to resist a claim on the grounds that one or more of the conditions are not fulfilled. As a condition precedent to doing so, he must give due notice of his grounds of objection.

2 Neighbourhood management powers

When an application has been made to the High Court for a

scheme for neighbourhood management powers, the landlord does not have to take any action on a tenant's notice to enfranchise beyond such as may seem reasonable to him (1967 Act, s 19 (14)). This in effect suspends the right to enfranchise until the application to the court has been determined. This has no effect on claims for extended leases.

3 Residential rights

After a tenant has given notice to enfranchise or claim an extended lease, the landlord may apply to the county court for possession of the house in order that he or a member of his family may occupy it (1967 Act, s 18). If he is successful, the tenant's claim is defeated, but he is entitled to compensation. The right to possession and the right to compensation arise on the same day, which is fixed subsequently.

The landlord will succeed if he can establish:

(a) that all or part of the house is or will be reasonably required for occupation as the only or main residence of himself or an adult member of his family. Members of the family for this purpose are: the landlord's spouse, his child, his child-in-law or his spouse's child (including illegitimate, adopted or step-child) over the age of eighteen, and his parent or parent-in-law. If the landlord's interest is held in trust, the residential occupation can be by a person having an interest under the trust (whether or not also a trustee), or an adult member of his family. The date at which the landlord must reasonably require the house is the date when the lease will come to an end, which may be some years distant, not the date of the court hearing (*Gurvidi* v *Mangat* (1972) 116 SJ 255);

(b) that his interest in the house was not purchased or created after 18 February 1966. Any interest which has merged in the landlord's, but which otherwise would have subsisted for at least five years longer than the tenancy, must also satisfy this test. For this purpose, the date of termination of any interest (including the tenancy) is its expiry date, or the earliest possible date on which it could be terminated by notice;

(c) that greater hardship would not be caused by the court's making the order than by refusing to make it. This is a matter entirely within the court's discretion. It must have regard to all the circumstances, including whether the landlord or the tenant has alternative accommodation available. This is equivalent to the discretion exercised when a landlord applies for permission on similar grounds under the Rent Act.

If an application for possession on these grounds, or on the grounds mentioned in the following section, is dismissed or withdrawn, the landlord may be prevented by court order from making a further application on either of the two grounds for five years from the date of the order (1967 Act, Sched 2, para 8 (3)). The court may make such an order where:

(a) the application was not made in good faith; or

(b) the landlord requested the tenant to deliver up possession without an application to the court, and attempted to support the request by misrepresentation or the concealment of material facts.

4 Redevelopment rights

Where an extended lease is granted to a tenant, or he has given notice claiming one, the landlord can apply to the county court for possession of the house for redevelopment (1967 Act, s 17). This does not apply where the tenant has given notice to enfranchise. The landlord must establish that for the purposes of redevelopment he proposes to demolish or reconstruct the whole or a substantial part of the premises. If the court is satisfied as to that, it must make an order giving the landlord possession, and declaring that the tenant is entitled to compensation. The two rights arise on the same day, which is fixed subsequently (see next section). The landlord's application may be made at any time, but not earlier than twelve months before the termination of the original tenancy.

The tenant can, with two exceptions, defeat the landlord's application by giving notice to enfranchise. If this happens, only an order for costs can then be made on the landlord's application to the court. The two exceptions are:

(a) if the tenant gives his notice on or after the date of the order fixing the date for the termination of the tenancy;

(b) if the landlord's application is made within twelve months after the tenant gave his notice claiming an extended lease.

The landlord may be barred from making an application on this ground when a previous application or approach to the tenant was made in bad faith (see the end of the previous section).

5 Compensation and possession

Compensation is payable to a tenant by a landlord who has obtained an order for possession on the ground of occupation as a residence for himself or a member of his family, or of redevelopment, or where a public authority obtains possession for redevelopment. It consists of the amount the house would be expected to realise in the open market when sold by a willing seller to a willing buyer (1967 Act, Sched 2, para 5). It is calculated as if the sale:

(a) is subject to the rights of anyone who will be entitled as against the landlord to retain possession on the termination of the tenancy, but otherwise with vacant possession;

(b) is subject to any subsisting incumbrances the burden of which fell on the tenant during the tenancy, but which will continue after it ends, but otherwise free from incumbrances;

(c) is subject to a restriction limiting the use of the premises to the use to which they have been put since the commencement of the tenancy, and precluding the erection of any new dwelling-house, or any other building not ancillary to the house as a dwelling-house;

(d) did not include any right to enfranchise under the 1967 Act;

(e) was of a tenancy which had been extended under the 1967 Act, if this has not already been done.

In default of agreement, the amount of compensation is determined by a leasehold valuation tribunal (1967 Act, s 21 (1) (c); 1980 Act, Sched 22, para 8 (1)). No compensation is payable for improvements where the tenancy was a business tenancy, as it would otherwise have been under the Landlord and Tenant

Act 1927, Pt I (1967 Act, Sched 2, para 6 (1)).

Compensation is payable on a date fixed by the court once the amount of it is known (1967 Act, Sched 2, para 2). This date is not earlier than the original term date of the tenancy, and, unless the court sees special reason to the contrary, will be at least four but not more than twelve months after the date of the order. In fixing the date, the court has regard to the conduct of the parties, including, in a redevelopment case, the extent of the landlord's preparations.

The order for possession terminates every immediate and derivative sub-tenancy (1967 Act, Sched 2, para 3; 1976 Act, Sched 8, para 18). Sub-tenants do not have the protection of the Rent Act, or the 1976 Act, where the letting to them was made after the landlord's application for possession (or, in a public authority case, the service on the tenant of the ministerial certificate). A sub-tenant is entitled to be heard on the landlord's application for possession. If the sub-tenancy is a business letting, so that on its termination the tenant is entitled to compensation under the 1954 Act, Pt II, the compensation is divided as may be just between the tenant and the sub-tenant (1967 Act, Sched 2, para 6 (2)). In case of dispute, the shares will be determined by the county court (1967 Act, s 20 (2) (d)).

The landlord is not concerned with the application of the compensation, except where it is capital money payable to trustees (1967 Act, Sched 2, para 7 (1)). The court may order that all or part of it shall be paid into court, to ensure that it is available for meeting charges on the tenant's interest, for dividing it or for any other purpose (1967 Act, Sched 2, para 2 (4)). Subject to that, the tenant's written receipt is a complete discharge to the landlord. Before paying, the landlord may deduct any rent, or other sum recoverable as rent, payable up to the date of the termination of the tenancy, and any sums due and payable by the tenant under or in respect of the tenancy or any collateral agreement.

Capital moneys may be used by trustees for paying this compensation, and money may be raised on mortgage for it under the Settled Land Act 1925, ss 71, 73, Law of Property Act 1925, s 28, and University and College Estates Act 1925, ss 26, 31 (1967 Act, Sched 2, para 9).

If either the landlord or tenant is guilty of any unreasonable delay or default, the county court may revoke or vary any previous order for costs, and direct repayment of sums previously paid under such an order (1967 Act, Sched 2, para 8).

C — Procedure by Tenant

1 Tenant's notice

A tenant who is qualified to enfranchise or claim an extended lease exercises that right by giving written notice to his landlord of his desire to have the freehold, or an extended lease (1967 Act, ss 8 (1), 14 (1)). The notice must clearly opt for one of the alternatives (*Byrnlea Property Investments Ltd* v *Ramsay* [1969] 2 QB 253). It must be in the prescribed form.

The particulars that must be included in the notice are (1967 Act, Sched 3, para 6 (1); 1980 Act, Sched 21, para 7):

(*a*) The address of the house, and particulars to identify the premises to which the claim extends;

(*b*) Identification of the instrument creating the tenancy;

(*c*) Details of the rateable value, showing that the house was at the material time within the rateable value limits, and that the tenancy is and was a tenancy at a low rent;

(*d*) The date at which the tenant acquired the tenancy;

(*e*) The periods during the preceding ten years, and since the acquisition of the tenancy, that the tenant has and has not occupied the house as his residence, with details of the parts of it not so occupied and of any other residence.

Where the tenant's claim is based upon occupation by one or more members of his family, a tenant for life under the Settled Land Act 1925, or a person entitled or permitted to occupy the house under some other settlement, the particulars on the form must include details to substantiate the claim (1967 Act, Sched 3, para 6 (2)).

2 Service

The tenant may serve his notice on any person having an interest in the house superior to his (ie, fee simple, superior tenancy and reversionary tenancy) and, where the claim is for enfranchisement, their mortgagee whose securities will be dis-

charged (1967 Act, Sched 3, paras 8, 9). The notice may also be
served on a mortgagee or receiver in possession of the landlord's interest. In the case of a debenture-holder's charge, only
the trustee or a receiver is entitled to notice. Where the occupier
is a sub-tenant, the recipient of the notice does not have to be
his immediate landlord, although it normally will be. The tenant
must serve copies of the notice on any other persons whom he
knows or believes to have an interest in the house superior to
his own.

Notices are served in accordance with the Landlord and
Tenant Act 1927, s 23 (1) (1967 Act, s 22 (5)).

3 Missing landlord

Where a tenant who wishes to enfranchise cannot find, or
cannot ascertain the identity of, his landlord, he may apply to
the High Court instead of serving notice (1967 Act, s 27). For
procedure, see *Re Robertson's Application* [1969] 1 WLR 109;
Re Frost's Application [1970] 1 WLR 1145. If, after steps have
been taken without success to trace the landlord, the court finds
that the tenant is entitled to enfranchise, it makes an order to
secure his rights to him. It designates a person to execute a
conveyance in his favour. The price and rent to date (limited to
six years' arrears: *Re Howell's Application* [1972] Ch 509)
ascertained by a surveyor selected by the President of the Lands
Tribunal is paid into court.

4 Sub-tenant claimant

Where the claiming tenant is a sub-tenant there are certain
consequential variations in procedure: see pp 147–9.

D — PROCEDURE BY LANDLORD

1 On receipt of notice

Anyone who receives a tenant's notice, or copy of it, must
forthwith serve a copy of it on anyone else he knows or believes
to have an interest in the house superior to that of the tenant
(including a mortgagee or receiver in possession), not already
named in the notice as one of the people who are to receive a
copy of it (1967 Act, Sched 3, para 8). The recipient of a notice,

or copy, who himself passes on a copy must add, on that copy, the names of anyone he serves to the list of persons to be served. He must also notify the tenant of the name(s) he has added.

If the recipient of the tenant's notice, or a copy of it, knows who is the person designated by the Act as 'reversioner', or believes that he himself is, he must give written notice to the tenant. He must also send copies of this notice to everyone he knows or believes to have an interest in the house superior to the tenant's. The Act designates a reversioner to cover the position of sub-tenancies, but the requirement for serving this notice seems to cover all cases. The reversioner is either the person entitled to the tenancy having an expectation of at least thirty years' possession most immediately expectant on the termination of the tenant's sub-tenancy, or if there is no such interest, the freeholder (1967 Act, Sched 1, para 2). The land-lord may require the tenant to pay a deposit of three times the annual rent or £25 (whichever is greater), to be deposited with him or his nominee as his agent or as stakeholder. He may also require the tenant to deduce his title and furnish a statutory declaration as to the particulars of the occupation of the house on which he relies (Regs, Sched, Pt I).

2 Delay

Failure or delay in complying with the provisions for serving the tenant's notice and copies of it, passing them on, and giving notice as to who is the reversioner, may involve liability for any loss it occasions. Anyone who fails to comply with the require-ments without reasonable cause, or who is guilty of unreason-able delay, will be liable for loss to the tenant or anyone with an interest superior to his (1967 Act, Sched 3, para 8 (3)).

3 Counter-notice

Within two months of the tenant's giving notice, the landlord must give a notice in reply in the prescribed form (1967 Act, Sched 3, para 7). This states whether or not the landlord admits the tenant's right to enfranchise or claim an extended lease. If he does not admit it, the grounds of opposition must be stated. Any question as to the correctness of the particulars of the house and premises given in the tenant's notice may be left open by the landlord. Any dispute as to whether the tenant is entitled to the rights is determined by the county court (1967 Act, s 20 (2) *(a)*).

If the landlord intends to apply for possession on the grounds that he requires the premises either for redevelopment, or for the occupation of himself or his family, he must say so in his reply. In any other case, a landlord who wishes to exercise his right to have any premises specified by the tenant excluded, or to include any other premises, must say so in his reply, or specifically reserve the rights.

The landlord's admission, in his reply, of the tenant's right to enfranchise or claim an extended lease is generally conclusive:

(a) that the tenant's tenancy is a long tenancy at a low rent; and

(b) that when he gave his notice, the tenant had been occupying the house as his residence for the last three years, or periods amounting to three years in the last ten.

The only exception is where the landlord shows that he was induced to make the admission by misrepresentation or concealment of material facts (1967 Act, Sched 3, para 7 (4)).

E — CONVEYANCING PROCEDURE

Detailed provisions, with time limits, for the conduct of the steps to complete the conveyance of the freehold or the grant of the extended lease are set out in the Schedule to the Regulations.

F — EFFECT OF TENANT'S NOTICE

1 Generally

When a notice to enfranchise is given, the landlord is bound to convey and the tenant is bound to accept (subject to a right to withdraw) a conveyance of the house (1967 Act, s 8 (1)). The details of how this works out are given in Chapter XVIII. When a tenant gives a notice claiming an extended lease, his landlord is bound to grant and he to accept a new tenancy (1967 Act, s 14 (1)). Details of the terms and other provisions relating thereto are given in Chapter XIX.

Once a notice is given, it is binding not only on the landlord and the tenant, but, to the extent that a contract would be, upon their executors, administrators and assigns (1967 Act, s 5). The tenant's rights cannot, however, be assigned separately from his tenancy. Accordingly, an assignment of the tenancy alone, or an assignment of his tenancy in part only of the house, will render the notice ineffective. The landlord is then entitled to compensation for any interference in his right to dispose of or deal with the house or any neighbouring property.

A tenant's notice is registrable as an estate contract, either by a notice or caution at the Land Registry, or as a land charge class C (iv) at the Land Charges Department. If the tenant gives notice of withdrawal, or the landlord is otherwise discharged from his obligations, the landlord may require the tenant to procure the cancellation of any registration (Regs, Sched)

If, before the tenant's notice is carried into effect, a notice to treat is served on either the landlord or tenant by a person or body with compulsory acquisition powers, the tenant's notice ceases to have effect. Compensation is, however, assessed and divided as if the notice were effective. A tenant can also render his own notice claiming an extended lease ineffective by subsequently serving a valid notice to enfranchise.

Where the landlord has contracted to dispose of his interest and the tenant then serves notice to enfranchise, the landlord and all other persons are discharged from further performance of that contract as far as it relates thereto. This applies even if the contract is made pursuant to a court order, but not if the contract provides for this eventuality. A tenant's notice claiming an extended lease only has this effect if both parties entered into the contract on the basis that vacant possession would or might be available on the termination of the existing tenancy.

2 Notice given by sub-tenant

If the tenant in possession is a sub-tenant this does not prejudice his position if he otherwise qualifies to enfranchise or claim an extended lease (1967 Act, Sched 1). All the superior interests have to be dealt with, but to simplify this one person is designated as 'reversioner'. He is the person entitled to the tenancy of the house most immediately in reversion to the claiming sub-tenant's, which gives him an expectation of at least thirty years' possession, or if none, the freeholder (1967 Act, Sched 1, para 2). For calculating the thirty years it is assumed that a tenancy other than one in possession will terminate on its term date. One in possession is assumed to terminate on whichever is later of the term date and the date the tenant serves his notice, unless the landlord has given notice to quit, in which case the date in the notice to quit is taken (1967 Act, Sched 1, para 13).

The reversioner is authorised and required to conduct the proceedings arising out of the notice. The county court has power in certain circumstances to appoint a different reversioner, and to remove and replace one who delays or defaults (1967 Act, Sched 1, para 3).

The reversioner can, in the name of the other landlords (ie, the others with interests superior to the claiming sub-tenant) and on their behalf, *inter alia* execute a conveyance or lease giving effect to the tenant's notice (other than on behalf of the owner of a Crown interest) and take and defend legal proceedings arising out of the notice (1967 Act, Sched 1, paras 4 (1), 14 (1)). Possession proceedings by a landlord on the ground of redevelopment, or for occupation by himself or his family, have to be taken by the landlord concerned (1967 Act, Sched 1, para 6 (1)). The reversioner's actions bind the other landlords. If some other landlord cannot be found, the reversioner must apply to the court for directions, but subject thereto, must proceed to give effect to the tenant's notice in the usual way, paying into court any sum due to the missing landlord (1967 Act, Sched 1, para 4 (2), (3)).

A reversioner acting in good faith and with reasonable care and diligence is not liable to any other landlords for any loss or damage caused by any act or omission in the exercise or intended exercise of his statutory authority (1967 Act, Sched 1, para 4 (4)). The other landlords are under a duty to give him all the information and assistance that he may require, including producing on completion all the deeds and documents required to perfect the tenant's title. In default, they must indemnify the reversioner against any liability he incurs as a consequence (1967 Act, Sched 1, para 5 (5), (6)). Each of the other landlords must make a just contribution to such of the reversioner's costs and expenses as he cannot or does not recover from the tenant.

Notwithstanding the reversioner's general authority, any other landlord may require to deal directly with the tenant on certain points. He may be separately represented in any legal proceedings concerning the title to his property, or the price payable on enfranchisement (1967 Act, Sched 1, para 5 (1)). On giving notice to the tenant and the reversioner, he may deal directly to deduce, evidence or verify his title, if he objects to disclosing it to the reversioner (and must deal directly if the tenant so requires, by notice to him and the reversioner), and also to agree the price payable for his interest on enfranchisement (1967 Act, Sched 1, para 5(2), (3); 1980 Act, Sched 22, para 10). Even if he does not do this, he may require the reversioner to apply to a leasehold valuation tribunal for it to determine the price. Finally, he may require that the part of the price payable to him shall be paid to him or his representative. But if, having been notified of arrangements for completion, he neither attends nor makes and notifies the reversioner of alternative arrangements to receive the money, the tenant can pay it to the reversioner on his behalf, and the reversioner's receipt will be a good discharge (1967 Act, Sched 1, para 5 (4)).

3 Other notices and proceedings

A tenant's notice to enfranchise or claim an extended lease renders the following ineffective while it is current:

   (a) a tenant's notice terminating the tenancy (1967 Act, Sched 3, para 1 (2));

   (b) a tenant's request for a new business tenancy and a tenant's notice that he does not desire a business tenancy to be continued (1954 Act, ss 26, 27 (1); 1967 Act, Sched 3, para 1 (3));

   (c) a landlord's notice terminating a long tenancy or a business tenancy (1954 Act, ss 4, 25; 1967 Act, Sched 3, para 2 (2)).

These notices, even if validly given, are cancelled by a tenant's notice under the 1967 Act. But if that claim is not effective, a new notice can be served under the 1954 Act, and the date specified for the termination of the tenancy can be either the date in the original notice, or three months from the giving of the new notice (whichever is later) (1967 Act, Sched 2, para 2 (3));

(d) termination of a tenancy by effluxion of time, by termination of a superior tenancy or by a landlord's notice to quit (1967 Act, Sched 3, para 3). This lasts for three months after the currency of the claim to enfranchise or for an extended lease. If the claim is ineffective, the tenancy will terminate at the end of three months, if, but for this provision, it would otherwise have terminated earlier;

(e) proceedings for re-entry or forfeiture brought without leave of the court (1967 Act, Sched 3, para 4). Leave is only to be granted when the court is satisfied that the tenant's claim was not made in good faith, and the tenant's claim then ceases to have effect. The court has granted leave where the tenant claiming to enfranchise has been convicted of using the premises as a brothel (*Central Estates (Belgravia) Ltd* v *Woolgar* [1972] 1 QB 48) and where the tenant claiming an extended lease had no prospect of complying with the repairing covenants that would have been included in it (*Liverpool Corporation* v *Husan* [1972] 1 QB 48).

4 Compensation for depreciation

Compensation for depreciation in the value of land by physical factors caused by the use of public works is normally available to tenants of the land concerned if there is at least three years of the lease unexpired (Land Compensation Act 1973, s 2 (4)). Service of notice to enfranchise or claim an extended lease, however, entitles the tenant to claim this compensation even before he acquires the freehold or the new lease (Land Compensation Act 1973, s 12). Also, after enfranchisement or the grant of the extended lease, but before disposing of the new interest so acquired, the tenant may still claim any compensation due to him as tenant under the original long lease.

G — PARTICULAR LANDLORDS

1 Under a disability

A receiver appointed under the Mental Health Act 1959, Pt VIII, for a landlord incapable of managing and administering his property and affairs by reason of mental disorder, or, if none, anyone authorised in that behalf, takes the place of the landlord for the purposes of the 1967 Act, under an order of the Court of Protection (1967 Act, s 26 (2)).

2 Ecclesiastical authorities

Church of England land is subject to claims for enfranchisement or extended leases to the same extent as land in private ownership. The Church Commissioners are, however, given special powers which enable them to supervise the arrangements where the landlord's interest belongs to a capitular body under the Cathedrals Measure 1963, without interfering with the tenant's rights. Their powers formerly extended to cases where the reversion belonged to an ecclesiastical benefice, but since the transfer of glebe land to the Diocesan Boards of Finance (Endowments and Glebe Measure 1976, s 15), that jurisdiction has lapsed. The Commissioners must (1967 Act, s 31 (2); 1980 Act, Sched 22, para 9):

(a) sanction the provisions in any conveyance of the freehold or in any extended lease, the price or rent payable, and the exercise of the landlord's right to claim possession for redevelopment, unless these matters are determined by the court, a leasehold valuation tribunal or the Lands Tribunal;

(b) sanction any agreement for compensation for giving possession for development which is made without an application to the court;

(c) sanction any grant of a tenancy in satisfaction of a tenant's right to an extended lease;

(d) be heard, if they wish, in any proceedings to which an ecclesiastical landlord is a party, or in which it is entitled to appear and be heard.

Money received on enfranchisement or by way of compensation is treated as part of the endowment of the cathedral church of which the house formed part (1967 Act, s 31 (3)). Where the landlord has to pay compensation for possession for redevelopment, it is paid out of moneys forming part of the endowment of the cathedral church available for investment.

3 Charities

Charities are in no special position under the 1967 Act. They must comply with its provisions for conveying the freehold or granting an extended lease when a tenant of theirs makes a valid claim.

4 Trustees

Although in general the provisions of the 1967 Act bind trustees, the special rules affecting them are dealt with below, in the next section.

5 Public authorities

Certain public authorities are to different extents exempted from the obligation to permit enfranchisement or grant extended leases. The details are given above, pp 135–7. They may also be in a position to reserve development rights (p 154).

6 Mortgagees in possession

A mortgagee in possession of the landlord's interest takes the place of the landlord in the procedure arising when a tenant gives notice to enfranchise or claiming an extended lease, and in claiming possession for redevelopment (1967 Act, s 25). The conveyance or extended lease may be executed by the landlord by the direction of the mortgagee, or by the mortgagee in the name and on behalf of the landlord. Any compensation paid to the tenant is added to the mortgage debt, although it does not fall within the mortgagor's personal covenant. Any compensation recovered from the tenant is dealt with as if it were the proceeds of a sale.

If a receiver is in receipt of the rents and profits, whether appointed by the court or the mortgagee, the landlord needs the mortgagee's approval before applying for possession for his own or his family's occupation, or for redevelopment (1967 Act, s 25 (5)). In such a case, the mortgagee may require, by written notice to the landlord, that the provisions relating to a mortgagee in possession shall apply.

H — Settled Property

The fact that either the landlord's interest or the tenant's interest in a house is subject to a settlement does not prevent a claim for enfranchisement or an extended lease.

Where it is the tenant's interest that is settled, the qualification of occupation of the house by the tenant as his residence is satisfied by the occupation of a person doing so under the trusts. This will be the sole tenant for life for the purposes of the Settled Land Act 1925, or, where the lease is vested in trustees, the person entitled or permitted to occupy the house under the trusts (1967 Act, s 6 (2), (3)). On the death of a person occupying the house by virtue of his interest under a trust, his relatives have similar rights to add his period of residence to their own as if he had been an absolute owner.

Where a new lease is granted to a Settled Land Act tenant for life, it is to be treated as a subsidiary vesting deed in accordance with s 53 (2) of the Act (1967 Act, s 6 (2) *(b)*).

Capital money may be used to defray the expenses of proceedings taken by a tenant for life, statutory owners or trustees for sale, for claiming enfranchisement or an extended lease, and money may be raised on mortgage for this purpose (1967 Act, s 6 (5)). The Settled Land Act 1925 and the Law of Property Act 1925, s 28, are extended for that purpose.

If the landlord's interest is settled, the trustees or tenant for life, as the case may be, are obliged to comply with the 1967 Act's requirements after service of a tenant's notice. On an enfranchisement, the payment received will be capital money (1967 Act, s 24 (1)). Where the landlord's interest is vested in a custodian trustee, the landlord for all the purposes of the 1967 Act, except executing any deed which is required, will be the managing trustee or committee of management (1967 Act, s 26 (1)).

I — Redevelopment Rights

There are a number of cases in which redevelopment rights can be retained by landlords whose tenants exercise rights under the 1967 Act. These are necessarily restricted, as to a greater or lesser extent they detract from the tenant's rights. The different possibilities are dealt with separately below.

1 General

The rights that all landlords have to regain possession for redevelopment after the tenant has claimed an extended lease are dealt with above, p 140. This does not apply after the tenant has enfranchised.

2 Covenants against redevelopment

Where the landlord is a local authority (county, district or London borough council, the Greater London Council, the Common Council of the City of London), the Development Board for Rural Wales, the Commission for the New Towns, a new town development corporation or a university body (as listed under *(d)* on page 136), it can have covenants inserted in the conveyance or extended lease reserving redevelopment rights to itself (1967 Act, s 29 (1), (2), (5), (6A), (8); Development of Rural Wales Act 1977, Sched 7, para 5). A university body may reserve rights for redevelopment by a related university body (1967 Act, s 29 (6B); 1980 Act, Sched 21, para 5). The landlord must own the freehold, and there must be no intermediate tenancy carrying an expectancy of as much as thirty years' possession (1967 Act, Sched 1, para 6 (2)). A university body must obtain the consent of the Secretary of State for Education and Science before requiring such covenants (1967 Act, s 29 (6)). The covenants restrict the tenant from carrying out development or clearing land, to such an extent as is necessary to reserve the land for possible development by the landlord.

If the land is subsequently compulsorily acquired, any increase in its value attributed to any development in breach of these covenants is ignored in assessing the compensation payable (1967 Act, s 29 (4)).

3 Pre-emption rights

Pre-emption rights can be reserved on an enfranchisement from, or the grant of an extended lease by, the Commission for the New Towns, the Development Board for Rural Wales, a new town development corporation and a council of a receiving district for overspill population under the Town Development Act 1952, s 5, and the Housing Act 1961, s 34 (1967 Act, s 30

(1), (2), (7); Development of Rural Wales Act 1977, Sched 7, para 5). The landlord concerned must be the freeholder, and there must not be any intervening tenancy giving an expectation of possession of as much as thirty years (1967 Act, Sched 1, para 6 (2)). The rights are reserved by inserting two covenants in the conveyance or lease. The first is that no tenancy of any part of the property may be granted without the landlord's consent. Where this covenant is in a lease the Landlord and Tenant Act 1927, s 19, does not apply. So there is no implied proviso that the landlord's consent cannot unreasonably be withheld (1967 Act, s 30 (5)). The second covenant gives the landlord the right of pre-emption on a sale of any part of the property. The price payable on the pre-emption ignores the diminution in the value attributable to the right of pre-emption, but also ignores any damage due to severance or disturbance (1967 Act, Sched 4, para 3 (5)).

4 Enforcement of covenants

Covenants entered into under either of sections 2 or 3 above are deemed registrable in the Land Charges Department or on the land register if they would not otherwise be, and are binding on successors in title accordingly (1967 Act, Sched 4, para 1). They cannot be varied under the Law of Property Act 1925, s 84, nor does the rule against perpetuities apply to them.

There is only one method of enforcement of these covenants (1967 Act, Sched 4, paras 1 (1), 2, 3). The authority in whose favour the covenant was made serves notice on the owner or tenant of the property. It alleges, and specifies, the breach of covenant, and states that unless a counter-notice is served within a specified period (at least six weeks) the authority will execute a vesting declaration in respect of that interest. If a counter-notice is served, no vesting declaration can be executed without leave of the court. There is a six-month period for executing the vesting declaration. This runs from the end of the period of service of the counter-notice, or its withdrawal, or from the date of the court order permitting its execution. The declaration vests the interest in the authority on the date it specifies. Compensation is payable, assessed under the Land Compensation Act 1961. In calculating it, no account is taken of damage from severance or disturbance, nor of the lowering effect of any pre-emption right under the 1967 Act.

5 Re-acquisition

A house enfranchised by purchase from the Commission for the New Towns, the Development Board for Rural Wales or a university body, in a case where a covenant against redevelopment was given by the tenant, may be re-acquired for redevelopment, otherwise than for investment, by the former landlord, or, in the case of a university body, a related university body (1967 Act, Sched 4, paras 4–6; Development of Rural Wales Act 1977, Sched 7, para 5 (5)). The Commission must have the authority of the Secretary of State for the Environment, the Board that of the Secretary of State for Wales. The Secretary of State for Education and Science carries out the compulsory re-purchase on behalf of a university body.

J — MANAGEMENT RIGHTS

Management rights in an area where the properties are occupied directly or indirectly on leases granted by one landlord can be granted to the landlord and/or a representative body of occupiers. If the scheme grants rights to the landlord, they attach to his interest. The applicant has first to obtain a certificate from the Secretary of State for the Environment (in Wales, the Secretary of State for Wales), and then make an application for approval of the scheme to the High Court.

The scheme may provide for all or any of the following, and may vary for different parts of the area (1967 Act, s 19 (6), (8)):

(a) for regulating the redevelopment, use or appearance of property;

(b) to empower the applicant to maintain or repair, and remedy any failure to comply with the scheme. The operation of the scheme may be conditional on the applicant's doing this;

(c) for imposing repair and maintenance obligations in respect of property owned or used in common;

(d) for allowing the applicant to inspect the property, and to recover sums due by a charge on the property. The applicant has the powers of enforcement of a mortgage by deed. To avoid building societies being prohibited from lending on the enfranchised properties, because their charge might not rank as a first charge (Building Societies Act 1962, s 32), the scheme should contain a provision postponing the charge arising under the scheme (*Re Abbots Park Estate (No 2)* [1972] 1 **WLR** 1597).

Examples of lessees' covenants that have been continued under a scheme are exterior repairs and fire insurance. Membership of a tenants' association can, in an appropriate case, be included as a requirement of a scheme (*Re Abbots Park Estate (No 1)* [1972] 1 **WLR** 598).

The application to the High Court has to be made within a year of the Secretary of State giving his certificate (1967 Act, s 19). The High Court must have regard primarily to the likely benefit to the area as a whole when considering the scheme. Architectural and historical considerations may also be taken into account. It may exclude part of an area, or refuse to sanction a scheme. It must generally, however, approve a scheme which is fair and practicable, and does not give a landlord a degree of control out of proportion to his previous powers, even if the landlord's powers under the scheme will exceed those exercised under the leases (*Re Dulwich College Estate's Application* (1973) 231 EG 845).

A Secretary of State's certificate, and a scheme when approved, are registrable as local land charges (1967 Act, s 19 (10)).

K — Exclusion of Rights

An agreement purporting to exclude or modify the right to enfranchise or claim an extended lease is to that extent void (1967 Act, s 23; 1980 Act, Sched 21, para 1 (2)). This applies whether or not the agreement is in the instrument creating the tenancy, and whenever it is made. Provisions terminating or surrendering the tenancy if rights are claimed, or imposing any penalty or disability in that event, are also avoided. The following agreements are, however, still valid:

    (*a*) a tenant acquiring a superior interest ·or extended lease on other than the statutory terms;

    (*b*) a landlord and tenant agreeing that the tenant's notice to enfranchise or claiming an extended lease shall cease to be binding, and excluding or restricting the tenant from serving a further notice for up to three years;

(c) fixing the amount of compensation payable under the 1967 Act.

Agreements which the tenant makes which may have the effect of surrendering his statutory rights can be set aside or varied by a court, unless they were entered into with the prior agreement of the court (1967 Act, s 23 (3)). This affects a tenant who is entitled to enfranchise or to an extended lease, who agrees to surrender his tenancy or acquire any superior interest or an extended lease. It also affects a tenant under an extended lease who agrees to surrender it after the landlord has claimed possession for redevelopment. The tenant may apply to bring the matter before the county court, but any court in which proceedings are brought against him on the agreement has jurisdiction. The court must consider whether the tenant was adequately recompensed for his statutory rights, and have regard to the situation and conduct of the parties.

Chapter XVIII
Enfranchisement

Statutes referred to in this chapter:
Leasehold Reform Act 1967: '1967 Act.'
Rentcharges Act 1977: '1977 Act.'
Housing Act 1980: '1980 Act.'

A — INTEREST CONVEYED

1 Appurtenant rights

The interest that the tenant acquires on enfranchisement is the freehold of the land concerned.

The interest is conveyed together with (1967 Act, s 10):

(*a*) the rights implied by the Law of Property Act 1925, s 62 (general words) and s 63 (all-estate clause), unless the tenant consents to their being excluded or restricted;

(*b*) such of the following rights as the landlord is capable of granting and as are necessary to secure to the tenant as nearly as may be rights which, at the date he served his notice, he enjoyed under the tenancy, any collateral agreement or any provision made on the severance of the house from other property in the tenancy:

(i) rights of support for all or any part of the building;

(ii) rights of access of light or air to all or any part of the building;

(iii) rights to the passage of water, gas or other piped fuel, to the drainage or disposal of water, sewage, smoke or fumes, or to the use or maintenance of pipes or other installations for those purposes;

(iv) rights to the use of cables and other installations for the supply of electricity, for the telephone or for the receipt, directly or by landline, of television and radio transmission;

(*c*) such rights of way over property not conveyed as the landlord is capable of granting, and as are necessary for the reasonable enjoyment of the house and premises as they

159

have been enjoyed during the tenancy in accordance with its provisions;

(d) the benefit of such restrictive covenants by the landlord affecting other property, as are necessary to secure the continuance of restrictions under the lease or any collateral agreement, and which materially enhance the value of the house and premises. This includes covenants which maintain the value that would otherwise deteriorate (*Le Mesurier* v *Pitt* (1972) 221 EG 979 (LT)). The landlord is entitled to limit his personal liability under such covenants to breaches for which he is responsible.

The tenant cannot require the inclusion of any covenant or right of way which is unreasonable in all the circumstances. In deciding this, there must be taken into account the date the tenancy commenced and subsequent changes affecting the suitability of its provisions at the time when the tenant serves his notice. Where the tenancy comprised a number of neighbouring houses, the interests of those affected because of their interest in the other houses must also be considered (1967 Act, s 10 (5)).

In the course of the conveyancing, either the landlord or the tenant can give notice to the other stating the rights of way and provisions relating to restrictive covenants that he requires, and calling upon the recipient to state his requirements (Leasehold Reform (Enfranchisement and Extension) Regulations 1967, Sched, Pt I).

2 Incumbrances

The interest is to be conveyed subject to the following, but to no other incumbrances (1967 Act, ss 8, 10):

(a) the tenant's tenancy, and interests derived directly or indirectly out of it;

(b) any incumbrance (including personal liabilities in respect of the ownership of land but not charged on it) on the tenant's interest, or on any interest derived directly or indirectly out of it;

(c) any rentcharge secured on the property, in so far as it does not exceed the rent payable under the tenancy (see further in the next section);

(*d*) burdens originating in tenure;

(*e*) burdens relating to the upkeep or regulation for the benefit of the locality of any land, building, structure, works, way or watercourse;

(*f*) such of the following rights for the benefit of other property as can exist in law, and are necessary to secure to the person interested in that other property as nearly as may be the rights which, at the date of the tenant's notice, he had under the tenancy, any collateral agreement or any provision made on the severance of the house from other property in the tenancy:

(i) rights of support for all or any part of any building;

(ii) rights of access of light or air to all or any part of any building;

(iii) rights to the passage of water, gas or other piped fuel, to the drainage or disposal of water, sewage, smoke or fumes, or to the use or maintenance of pipes or other installations for those purposes;

(iv) rights to the use of cables or other installations for the supply of electricity, for the telephone or for the receipt, directly or by landline, of radio and television transmission;

(*g*) such rights of way as are reasonably necessary for the reasonable enjoyment of other property in which the landlord has an interest when the tenant serves his notice;

(*h*) rights of way granted, or agreed to be granted, by the landlord or the person then entitled to the reversion on the tenancy, before the tenant serves his notice;

(*i*) such provisions as the landlord may require to secure that the tenant is bound by restrictive covenants affecting the house and premises, otherwise than under the tenancy or any collateral agreement, or to indemnify the landlord against breaches of them;

(*j*) such restrictive covenants relating to the use of the house and premises as the landlord may require to secure the continuance of restrictions arising under the tenancy or any collateral agreement, which are capable of benefiting other property and of materially enhancing its value if only enforceable by the landlord;

(*k*) such further restrictive covenants as the landlord may

require which will not interfere with the reasonable enjoyment of the house and premises as they were enjoyed during
the tenancy, but will materially enhance the value of other
property in which the landlord has an interest;
    (*l*) any scheme of management rights approved by the
High Court (1967 Act, s 19 (10)).
The landlord cannot require the inclusion of any right of way
or restrictive covenant which would be unreasonable in all the
circumstances. This is considered in the light of the date of the
old tenancy, and the subsequent changes affecting the suitability
of its provisions at the date of the tenant's notice. Where the
tenancy comprised a number of neighbouring houses, the effect
on those interested in the other houses must also be considered
(1967 Act, s 10 (5)).

3 Rentcharges

Rentcharges to which the land to be conveyed is subject are
covered by special rules (1967 Act, s 11; 1977 Act, Sched 1,
para 4). These are based on two principles. First, if the rentcharge exceeds the rent payable under the tenancy at the date
the tenant serves his notice, the landlord is responsible for
procuring the release of it, at least to the extent of that excess.
He can apply for its compulsory apportionment or redemption
(1977 Act, ss 4, 8). So after enfranchisement, the tenant is
subject to no greater burden than before. Secondly, and subject
to that first principle, the tenant must take the land subject to
any subsisting rentcharge, unless the landlord decides at his
option to have the house released from it. Such a release will
increase the price that the tenant has to pay.

In considering whether the rentcharge exceeds the rent payable under the tenancy, one disregards any part of the rentcharge:
    (*a*) charged on or apportioned to other land, in such a
manner as to give the remedies provided by the Law of
Property Act 1925, s 190 (2), against that other land, and
    (*b*) in respect of which the landlord is entitled to be
exonerated or indemnified, provided these rights will pass to
the tenant.
The rent with which the rentcharge is to be compared is that

payable when the tenant serves his notice. But one must disregard any reduction because of damage to the property, any penal addition because of any breach of any of the terms of the tenancy or any collateral agreement. Only rent proper is taken into account, not payments for services, repairs, maintenance and insurance that may be reserved as rent. If the rent extends to property not enfranchised, a just apportionment must be made.

If there is any difficulty in redeeming the rentcharge, the amount agreed to be paid for redemption, or in default of agreement the price specified in redemption instructions under the 1977 Act, s 9 (4), may be paid into court. The tenant may, and if the landlord requires must, before the execution of the conveyance pay into court a sum up to the amount needed to redeem on account of the sum due to him on enfranchisement. If more is needed to redeem than the tenant is due to pay, the landlord must make up the difference. Where a sub-tenant is claiming to enfranchise, these redemption moneys come from the landlord who is under the obligation to pay, not (unless he is the one liable) from the reversioner (1967 Act, Sched 1, para 7 (2)). Once the total amount is paid in, and the conveyance is executed, the rentcharge is redeemed and claims for the redemption money lie only against the fund in court.

If the rentcharge affects other property, in addition to that being enfranchised, and no amount has been agreed or specified as the redemption price, the sum to be paid in shall be the amount certified by the apportioning authority pending apportionment on an application under s 4 of the 1977 Act as suitable provision, with a reasonable margin.

B — PRICE

1 General

There are different formulae for calculating the price of lower and higher value houses. These are dealt with separately below. If notice to enfranchise is given by a sub-tenant, a separate price is paid for each of the superior interests, each determined on those principles (1967 Act, Sched 1, para 7 (1) (b)). There is a separate method of calculation for 'minor superior tenancies'

(1967 Act, Sched 1, para 7A; 1980 Act, Sched 21, para 6).

The price cannot be increased by reason of a transaction since 15 February 1979, which involves the creation or transfer of a superior interest, whether or not preceding the claiming tenant's, nor of an alteration since then of the terms on which such an interest is held (Leasehold Reform Act 1979, s 1).

Even if it is agreed that the tenant shall pay nothing, or only a nominal sum, he is nevertheless deemed for all purposes to be a purchaser for valuable consideration in money or money's worth (1967 Act, s 8(5)).

If the price is not agreed, it is determined by a leasehold valuation tribunal (1967 Act, s 21 (1) *(a)*; 1980 Act, Sched 22, para 8 (1)). But before an application can be made to a tribunal, one of two preliminary requirements must have been satisfied (1967 Act, s 21 (1A); 1980 Act, Sched 22, para 8 (2)). Either the landlord must have informed the tenant of the price he is asking; or, if he has not done so, it must be at least two months after the tenant served his notice claiming to enfranchise.

2 Lower value houses

This section applies to houses with rateable values not exceeding £1,000 in Greater London or £500 elsewhere (taking into account any adjustment for improvements).

The price that the tenant pays the landlord is calculated as follows. It is the amount that the house would fetch in the open market at the date the tenant serves his notice, if sold by a willing seller, on the following assumptions (1967 Act, s 9 (1)):

(a) that the vendor sells a fee simple subject to the tenant's tenancy, and if he has not claimed an extended lease, subject to the extended lease that he would be entitled to claim;

(b) that the right to enfranchise does not exist;

(c) that the purchaser is to be exonerated until the end of the tenancy from any liability or change in respect of incumbrances on the interest of the tenant, or any interest derived directly or indirectly out of the tenancy;

(d) that, subject to the assumptions above, the sale is on the terms that will be included in the conveyance. If a scheme of management rights affects the value, this must be

reflected in the price (1967 Act, s 19 (10) *(b)*);

(e) that the tenant and members of his family residing with him in the house are not seeking to buy (Housing Act 1969, s 82).

The first dispute on price to reach the Court of Appeal was *Official Custodian for Charities* v *Goldridge* [1973] EGD 364. For cases where the reversion was not distant, it adopted the following valuation procedure.

The current ground rent for the remainder of the subsisting term is capitalised on the seven per cent table. The modern ground rent is then derived from the capital value of the site using the six per cent table, and that rent is capitalised using the six per cent table, allowance being made for its delayed receipt. The two capitalisation figures together give the price.

Where the reversion is distant the Lands Tribunal initially held that it was unnecessary to take the valuation beyond the stage of capitalising the current ground rent, on the assumption that an investor would view it as if it were payable in perpetuity. The valuation adopted has been ten times the ground rent (*Jenkins* v *Bevan-Thomas* (1972) 116 SJ 333). In a later case, the capitalisation of the current ground rent was augmented by a value placed on the reversion (*Mimmack* v *Solent Land Investments Ltd* [1973] EGD 635 (LT)).

In principle, all cases should be determined on evidence of what an investor could be expected to pay.

3 Higher value houses

These provisions apply to 1974 cases, houses with rateable values (adjusted, if appropriate, for improvements) exceeding £1,000 in Greater London and £500 elsewhere.

The price is still based on the open market price on a sale by a willing seller on the date the tenant serves his notice, but the assumptions to be applied are different (1967 Act, s 9 (1A); Housing Act 1974, s 118 (4)). They are:

(a) that the vendor sells a fee simple subject to the tenant's tenancy;

(b) that when that tenancy ends the tenant will be entitled to the benefit of Pt I of the Landlord and Tenant Act 1954 (long tenancy control);

(c) that the tenant neither has, nor will have, any repairing, maintenance or redecoration liability;

(d) that the right to enfranchise does not apply;

(e) that the price is diminished by the value of any improvement made at his own expense by the tenant or any predecessor in title;

(f) that the purchaser is to be exonerated until the end of the tenancy from any liability or charge in respect of incumbrances on the interest of the tenant, or any interest derived directly or indirectly out of the tenancy;

(g) that, subject to the assumptions above, the sale is on the terms that will be included in the conveyance. If a scheme of management rights affects the value, this must be reflected in the price.

The principal variations between the two formulae are that in the higher value cases it is assumed that at the end of the original long lease the tenant will remain in possession at a fair rent rather than at a ground rent, and in these cases the tenant's bid (the effect on the price of the tenant competing to buy) is not excluded. These factors should increase the price payable, although there has been a case where the ground rent under an extended lease has exceeded what the fair rent would have been (*Carthew* v *Estates Governors of Alleyn's College of God's Gift* (1974) 231 EG 809 (LT)).

In the first reported decision of the Lands Tribunal interpreting this formula, the price assessed was: the value of the landlord's interest subject to the long lease, plus half of the difference between the value of the house freehold in possession on the one hand and the aggregate value of the current separate freehold and leasehold interests on the other (*Norfolk* v *Trinity College, Cambridge* (1976) 278 EG 421 (LT)). That is, the landlord receives half of the gain made by merging the freehold and the leasehold. The value of improvements made by the tenant must be excluded from the figures.

4 Minor superior tenancies

This valuation formula applies to a superior tenancy with an expectation of possession not exceeding one month, and enjoying a profit rent of no more than £5 a year (1967 Act, Sched 1, para 7A; 1980 Act, Sched 21, para 6).

The price payable is to be:

$$£\frac{R}{Y} - \frac{R}{Y(1+Y)^n}$$

Where:

R is the profit rent, ie, the rent payable to the owner of the minor superior tenancy, less the rent payable by him;

Y is the yield (expressed as a decimal fraction) from 2½ per cent Consolidated Stock. The price of the stock is taken as the middle market price at the close of the last trading day in the week before the tenant gives notice of his claim to enfranchise;

n is the period in years (treating any part of a year as a whole year) which the minor tenancy would have to run if not extinguished by enfranchisement.

5 Costs

The tenant is also liable to pay the reasonable costs incurred in pursuance of the notice of or incidental to the following (1967 Act, s 9 (4)):

(a) the landlord's investigation of his right to enfranchise;

(b) any conveyance or assurance of any outstanding estate or interest in the house and premises;

(c) deducing, evidencing and verifying the title to any estate or interest in the house and premises;

(d) making out and furnishing such abstracts and copies as the tenant requires;

(e) any valuation of the house and premises.

This liability is cancelled if a subsequent notice to treat nullifies the tenant's notice. Costs which a contract could not provide that a purchaser must pay are not included.

The tenant does not have to pay the landlord's costs of a reference to a leasehold valuation tribunal (1980 Act, Sched 22, para 5).

6 Vendor's lien

The landlord has a vendor's lien on completion for the price, and this extends to any sums payable to him for rent or otherwise under the tenancy or any collateral agreement, up to the date of the conveyance, and for the costs of enfranchisement (1967 Act, s 9 (5)).

C — THE CONVEYANCE

1 Contents

The conveyance of the freehold to the tenant will contain the provisions necessary to define the interest conveyed. Where one party is given the right to require the inclusion of certain provisions, eg, restrictive covenants, the other party cannot object to any suggested provision that complies with the statutory requirements (*Le Mesurier* v *Pitt* (1972) 221 EG 979 (LT)). The conveyance will also state the price and contain the following provisions:

  (*a*) such covenant for title by the landlord as is implied by his being expressed to convey as trustee or mortgagee (Law of Property Act 1925, s 76 (1) (F); 1967 Act, s 10 (1));

  (*b*) a statutory acknowledgment in respect of any document of title the landlord retains, but no undertaking for its safe custody (Law of Property Act 1925, s 64; 1967 Act, s 10 (6));

  (*c*) covenants by the tenant restricting development or giving pre-emption rights in appropriate cases (1967 Act, ss 29 (1), 30 (1)).

Any dispute as to the contents of a conveyance on enfranchisement is determined by the county court (1967 Act, s 20 (2) (*b*)). By agreement, or when some other dispute concerning the same transaction has been referred to it, a leasehold valuation tribunal also has jurisdiction (1967 Act, s 21 (2) (*a*); 1980 Act, Sched 22, para 8 (3)).

2 Effect

A conveyance on enfranchisement has the same effect as any other conveyance of a freehold, with the following additions:

  (*a*) it overreaches any incumbrance capable of being overreached on a sale of settled land (Law of Property Act 1925, s 2 (1); 1967 Act, s 8 (4) (*a*));

(b) it releases the property conveyed from any rent-charge formerly charged on it, where the money to redeem it has been paid into court (1967 Act, s 11 (5));

(c) it discharges the property conveyed from any charge and any court order to enforce a charge, and extinguishes any term of years created for the purpose of a charge, without the persons entitled to or interested in the charge being parties to or executing the conveyance (1967 Act, s 12 (1)).

D — Mortgages of Landlord's Interest

1 Generally

As stated above, the conveyance on enfranchisement discharges the property from any charge on the landlord's interest (1967 Act, s 12 (1) (2)). The only exception to this is if the tenant does not pay the price in discharge of the charge or into court. The property remains charged to the extent of his default.

Where the landlord's interest is charged, the tenant must apply the price payable by him in discharge of the charges in accordance with their priorities. The tenant may pay the whole or part of the price into court if (1967 Act, s 13 (1), (2)):

(a) there is any difficulty in determining the sum due, or in ascertaining or finding the person entitled;

(b) the person entitled refuses or fails to make out a title, to accept payment or give a proper discharge, or to take any step reasonably required of him;

(c) the sum cannot be tendered without incurring or involving unreasonable cost or delay by reason of complications in title, the want of two or more trustees, or other reasons.

In determining the priority of the charges, the following rules apply (1967 Act, s 12 (3), (5), (7)):

(a) the chargee shall not exercise any right to consolidate with a separate charge on other property;

(b) if the chargee is the landlord or the tenant, the charge ranks in priority as it would have done, had that not been so;

(c) a charge (called 'a debenture-holder's charge') in

favour of the holders of a series of debentures issued by a company or other body of persons, or in favour of trustees for them, which at the date of the conveyance is a floating charge which has not crystallised, shall be disregarded, and the tenant shall make no payment in respect of it;

(d) if the chargee joins in the conveyance to release the property without payment, or for less than is due to him, effect is to be given to that.

The tenant may also be required to pay the price into court if written notice is given to him before the execution of the conveyance (1967 Act, s 13 (3)). This may be on the grounds of protecting the rights of the person entitled to the charge, by reason of an application to the court concerning a mortgage subsisting before the 1967 Act was passed, the bankruptcy or winding up of the landlord, or the enforcement of the charge by proceedings or the appointment of a receiver. Where proceedings are pending in a court other than a county court, and that court is specified in the notice, payment is made into that court.

In every case of payment into court of the whole of the price, any sum paid to redeem a rentcharge is deducted first (1967 Act, s 13 (4)).

A tenant claiming to enfranchise by virtue of a tenancy granted after 1 January 1968 must redeem a mortgage on the landlord's estate even if the tenancy was not authorised by the mortgagee when it should have been (1967 Act, s 12 (8)).

A mortgagee can be required to accept a minimum of three months' notice to pay off all or any part of the principal money secured, with interest to the date of repayment (1967 Act, s 12 (4)). This applies notwithstanding anything to the contrary in the mortgage instrument. The mortgagee is, however, additionally entitled, if he so requires, to receive a reasonable sum to cover the cost of reinvestment, other incidental costs and expenses, and any reduction in the rate of interest obtainable on reinvestment.

Although the property will be discharged under these provisions, even if the price payable on enfranchisement does not cover the mortgage debt, the personal covenants in the mortgage deed (including those of any guarantor) continue in force (1967 Act, s 12 (6)).

2 Mortgagees in possession

The procedure to be followed when a mortgagee is in possession of the landlord's interest is dealt with on p 152.

3 Transitional relief

The impact of the 1967 Act on the interests of landlords may create difficulties where those interests have been mortgaged, as the price payable on enfranchisement will often be less than the sum at which the landlord's interest would previously have been valued. Accordingly, special transitional provisions are made. They apply where on 27 October 1967 the house was held on a long lease terminating (or terminable by the landlord) within twenty years, and the interest of any landlord was charged, even though the landlord is under no personal liability (1967 Act, s 36).

An application can be made to the county court, or any other court to which application to enforce the charge has been made, if:

    (a) the landlord proposes during the tenancy (including any extended lease) to sell or realise any property charged;
    (b) the tenant gives notice to enfranchise; or
    (c) the person entitled to the charge takes any steps to enforce it or demand payment during the tenancy (including any extended lease).

The application can be made by the landlord or anyone entitled to a charge ranking in priority after the one concerned. The landlord may ask for the discharge or modification of the liabilities under the charge, and its terms, or for a restriction on the exercise of any right or remedy under it. A chargee may ask for the discharge or modification of the terms of a prior charge, or a restriction on the exercise of any right or remedy under it. Any order may be conditional, and may require the payment of money.

E — Tenant's Right to Withdraw

At any time up to one month after the price payable on enfranchisement has been agreed or determined, the tenant may give the landlord written notice that he is unable to proceed at the price he must pay (1967 Act, s 9 (3); 1980 Act, Sched 21, para 1 (2)). A sub-tenant claiming to enfranchise cannot give such a notice in respect of one only of the interests superior to his, but only in respect of all of them (1967 Act, Sched 1, para 9). The notice has the effect of cancelling the tenant's notice to enfranchise, and making him liable to pay compensation to the landlord. This compensation is the amount which is just to cover any interference caused by the original notice with the exercise of the landlord's power to dispose of or deal with the house and premises or any neighbouring property.

Giving a notice to withdraw prevents the tenant giving another notice to enfranchise for a further three years.

Chapter XIX
Extended Leases

Statutes referred to in this chapter:
Leasehold Reform Act 1967: '1967 Act.'
Housing Act 1980: '1980 Act.'

A — TERMS OF LEASE

1 Property

The premises comprised in the new lease are those in the tenant's existing lease, adjusted, if appropriate, as explained above, pp 137–8 (1967 Act, ss 2, 14 (1)).

2 Term of years

The new lease is for a term of fifty years from the term date of the existing lease (1967 Act, s 14 (1)). Accordingly, the new lease may be reversionary when granted.

3 Rent

The rent is a ground rent. This is defined as the letting value of the site (excluding the buildings on it) for the permitted uses to which the premises have actually been put during the existing tenancy, excluding any use only permitted with the landlord's consent (1967 Act, s 15 (2)). This letting value is calculated as at the date of commencement of the new lease, and is to be ascertained not earlier than twelve months in advance. In *Carthew* v *Estates Governors of Alleyn's College of God's Gift* (1974) 231 EG 809, the Lands Tribunal fixed ground rents of six per cent of site value (itself forty per cent of the total value of houses in Dulwich, South London), notwithstanding that those rents exceeded what would have been assessed as fair rents for the houses under the Rent Act.

If a fair rent is registered under the Rent Act for the premises, that registered rent is the maximum payable by the tenant under the extended lease until the landlord takes action (1967 Act, s 16 (1A); 1980 Act, Sched 21, para 4). What the landlord has to do is to serve written notice on the tenant that the registered rent no longer applies. It then ceases to be the maximum at the end of the rental period during which the notice was served. The landlord does not have to apply to cancel the registration.

If the terms of the extended lease put on the landlord any obligations to provide services, or for repairs, maintenance or insurance payment for these is in addition to the rent (1967 Act, s 15 (3)). If the existing tenancy has no provision for such a payment, or makes a fixed sum payable, the amount to be added is what is just, related to the cost from time to time to the landlord. This is determined at the same time as the letting value which represents the basic rent.

In default of agreement, the rent is determined by a leasehold valuation tribunal (1967 Act, s 21 (1) *(b)*; 1980 Act, Sched 22, para 8 (1)).

The rent may be revised at the end of twenty-five years from the term date of the original tenancy, at the landlord's option. The landlord must claim this by written notice within twelve months before any revised rent would take effect.

Where the new lease does not start until after the term date of the original tenancy, and the new rent and/or payment for services, etc, are greater than the old, an additional sum is payable by the tenant (1967 Act, s 15 (6)). This extra sum is the amount by which those payments and rent are higher, for the period from the term date, or the date of the tenant's notice (if later), until the beginning of the new lease.

4 Terms and conditions

The terms and conditions on which the new lease is granted are, subject to any agreement between the parties, the same as in the old one (including any collateral agreement), with these modifications (1967 Act, s 15 (1), (4), (5), (8)):

    (a) any necessary to take into account the exclusion of any property from the new lease, or any alteration to the property since the old lease was granted;

    (b) any necessary where the tenant was entitled to more than one old tenancy from the same landlord and the new lease combines their effect;

(*c*) any option to renew or purchase, and right of pre-emption, is excluded;

(*d*) any provision for premature determination, other than on the breach of the terms of the tenancy, must be excluded;

(*e*) having regard to changes since the grant of the old tenancy, any provision that would be unreasonable if unchanged must be modified or excluded;

(*f*) the new lease must provide that no sub-tenancy granted out of it, whether immediately or not, and even if a long tenancy, confers any right against the landlord to enfranchise or claim an extended lease;

(*g*) a right must be reserved to the landlord to resume possession for the purposes of redevelopment;

(*h*) where appropriate a tenant's covenant restricting redevelopment or giving the landlord a right of pre-emption is to be included.

The extended lease may contain a statement that it is granted pursuant to the 1967 Act. Unless the statement appears from the lease to be untrue, it is conclusive evidence of that fact as against anyone not a party to it (1967 Act, s 16 (7), (8)). It is an offence to include such a statement in a lease, or execute it, knowing it to be untrue, or to use such a lease with intent to deceive. On indictment, an offender is liable to imprisonment for up to two years, or on summary conviction to imprisonment for up to three months, or to a fine of up to £100, or both.

5 Landlord's covenants

No covenant for title may be required from the landlord, beyond that implied in the grant, and he may limit his personal liability under any other covenant to breaches for which he is responsible (1967 Act, s 15 (9)).

B — COSTS AND EXPENSES

The tenant is responsible for paying the costs and expenses involved by reason of his claim to an extended lease. These include (1967 Act, s 14 (2)) the reasonable costs of or incidental to:

(*a*) the landlord's investigation of the tenant's right to an extended lease;

(b) the extended lease;

(c) any valuation obtained by the landlord to fix the rent payable under the extended lease.

Before the tenant can require the execution of the new lease, he must tender (1967 Act, s 14 (3)):

(a) all rent due to the date of tender;

(b) the costs payable, as above;

(c) any other sums due from the tenant to the landlord.

If the sum is not fully ascertained, the tenant may offer reasonable security instead.

C — Title

The landlord need not acquire a better title than he has or can require to have vested in him (1967 Act, s 14 (7)). No prohibition or restriction on sub-letting prevents the grant of an extended lease (1967 Act, Sched 1, para 12). The fact that the existing long tenancy was granted without the consent of the landlord's mortgagee, and is not binding on him, does not prejudice the tenant's right to an extended lease, unless the tenancy was granted after 1 January 1968 (1967 Act, s 14 (4)). In that exceptional case, any extended lease is not binding on the mortgagee. The extended lease is otherwise deemed to be authorised by and binding upon the chargees on the landlord's title.

Where the landlord's interest is in mortgage, and the mortgagee is entitled to possession of the deeds, the landlord must give him the counterpart of the extended lease within a month after its execution (1967 Act, s 14 (5), (6)). In default, he is deemed to be in breach of the terms of the mortgage. Where the tenant's subsisting lease is in mortgage, he must similarly deliver his new lease to his mortgagee within a month of its being granted.

D — Effect

On the grant of an extended lease, the following rights no longer apply (1967 Act, s 16 (1), (4), (6); Rent (Agriculture) Act 1976, Sched 8, para 17)):

(a) the right to enfranchise, unless the tenant gives his

notice to enfranchise before the term date of the original tenancy;

(b) the right to claim an extended lease (whether for the tenant or any sub-tenant);

(c) the controls applying to long tenancies and to business tenancies;

(d) sub-tenants deriving title whether immediately or derivatively do not, when the extended lease comes to an end, have any rights under the controls relating to long tenancies, business tenancies, or agricultural tied cottages, or as regulated tenants. A person granting a sub-tenancy to which this applies must inform the prospective sub-tenant.

An extended lease may comprise not only the house but also appurtenant premises. Although no second extended lease (or, where notice is given after the end of the original lease, enfranchisement) can be claimed in respect of the house, those other premises can be included in a claim relating to another house. If the landlord objects to the inclusion of those additional premises, they will be excluded (1967 Act, s 16 (2), (3)).

E — Claims by Sub-tenants

Where a sub-tenant claims an extended lease, it is granted by the first superior landlord who has a sufficiently long interest (1967 Act, Sched 1, para 10). Any intermediate tenancies are deemed to have been surrendered and regranted (with exceptions dealt with in the next paragraph). It may be necessary for more than one landlord to grant the lease, if no single one has a sufficient interest in the whole of the premises comprised in the tenant's notice. In such a case, the landlords grant the lease as if they were jointly entitled to their interests. All the superior landlords are included in the definition of 'landlord' for the purposes of fixing the rent payable under the new lease.

In certain cases, intermediate tenancies will or may be eliminated on the grant of the extended lease (1967 Act, Sched 1, para 11). Any superior tenancy which is vested in the tenant claiming the extended lease, or a trustee for him, is surrendered without any regrant. Where the effect of the new lease is to put any superior landlord in the position that the rent he receives is only £4 a year more than the rent he pays, or less (including a case where he pays more than he receives), he may surrender his interest. This he does by written notice to his immediate landlord and the reversioner. By a similar notice, any landlord may require that the lease shall confer on him a right to surrender if a revision of the rent under the extended lease subsequently puts him in that position. Should the landlord who ought to grant the new lease drop out by virtue of these provisions, he is replaced by the next superior landlord.

F — Excluding Subsequent Enfranchisement

With the approval of the court, a tenant entitled to enfranchise or to an extended lease may be granted a new tenancy in satisfaction of his rights, and that new tenancy may exclude the right to enfranchise (1967 Act, s 23 (4)–(7)). If the lease contains a statement to that effect, it is conclusive in favour of anyone not a party to it, unless it appears from the lease to be untrue. To include such a statement in a lease knowing it to be untrue, or to execute the lease or to make use of it with intent to deceive is an offence. On conviction on indictment an offender is liable to imprisonment for up to two years, and on summary conviction to imprisonment for up to three months, or to a fine of up to £100, or both.

Such a tenancy is on such terms as the court approves (1967 Act, s 23 (4), (5)). Subject to the consents required by charities when granting leases, and to the provisions of the 1967 Act relating to ecclesiastical landlords, the landlord is authorised to grant the lease. It is binding on all persons interested in his estate, except where the existing tenancy was granted after the Act's enfranchisement provisions came into force, and was not authorised by the landlord's mortgagee when it should have been, in which case the new tenancy is not binding on the mortgagee either. Such a lease has the effect of an extended lease granted as a result of a tenant's claim, unless it otherwise provides.

Index

Sub-tenant — *continued*
  protected shorthold tenancy, 45
  protection of, 19–20
    farmworkers' house, 79
    long tenancy, on termination of, 19–20
  shared accommodation with tenant, 60
Suitable alternative accommodation — *see* Alternative
    accommodation

TEMPORARY ACCOMMODATION, 93
  possession, recovery of, 98
Tied cottage —
  eviction, protection from, 113–15
  possession, grounds for —
    agricultural unit, premises required for person farming,
      27
    alternative accommodation, suitable, provision of, 23
    amalgamation scheme, 26
    employee, required for, 26
  rent allowance, calculation, 125
  statutory tenancy —
    rent, 8
    transmission on death, 18

UNFIT PREMISES —
  possession, grounds for, 28
University — *see also* Students
  landlord, as, 5–6, 136, 154, 156

WATER RATES —
  housing association tenancy rent, variation with, 87, 88